Scrum

The Definitive Guide for Professional
Scrum Master

*(Learn and Master Essential Scrum With This
Complete Scrum Guide)*

Sharon Holman

Published By   **Elena Holly**

Sharon Holman

*Scrum: The Definitive Guide for Professional
Scrum Master (Learn and Master Essential Scrum
With This Complete Scrum Guide)*

ISBN   978-1-77485-519-5

No part of this guidebook shall be reproduced in any form without permission in writing from the publisher except in the case of brief quotations embodied in critical articles or reviews.

Legal & Disclaimer

Table of Contents

Introduction

Complex products require considerable effort to create, produce and maintain. In the past, products would be created using project planning techniques that required a documented justification of the product as well as a the project plan. These documents were written by the manager of the project, and do not require the involvement of the team working on the project. Every aspect of the project such as the timeline for it, the budget and allocation of teamwork will be recorded and estimated by the management.

These plans covered the entire project from beginning to finish , with either the customer or company receiving results or a demo after the project was completed. This is not only dangerous, time-consuming, and expensive for the company, but the requirements of customers and hardware are constantly changing in the current. So the product that is delayed by about a year to complete its debut could be obsolete before even getting to show.

For the company that is creating the product, this could mean cost-intensive rework due to developers not receiving timely feedback and must incorporate new versions to bring the product up-to-date. All of this puts the developers under pressure to work extra hours. When employees are stressed, they usually get sluggish due to a lack of enthusiasm and energy. It could lead to the team members could quit or experience burnout.

Scrum is an improved method of managing the development, delivery and sustainability of complicated processes and products. The book will go over Scrum's Scrum structure, which covers the process of working as well as the steps needed for mastering Scrum, the Scrum framework, as well as some common mistakes when implementing Scrum.

Chapter 1: Agile Project Management

Perhaps the best way to begin is to state that you must remain alert. You must, indeed. Being agile is being active, energetic and productive. When you first heard "agile" in your first conference in business conference on software development and management What was your initial reaction? Confusion? Bewilderment? Something that is related to your high school psychology? You're certainly not the only one with this kind of confusion. of confusion and speculation.

What do you think? Agile can be described as a program for managing projects which aims to help businesses to achieve their goals in very short periods of time. It is important to be aware of Biblical Israelites who wasted a precious and valuable years traveling across Egypt towards in the Canaan Land. The historians have told us that the wandering Israelites were able to spend 40 years traveling which normally would have taken about 40 days. This is insanely insignificant?

Perhaps, it is a tale that best can be described as an untruth.

In our constantly changing world, shaped by the influence technological advancements, it is possible to face many challenges that the corporate world faces that make it increasingly difficult for companies to guarantee the loyalty of customers and resolve support issues and meet the needs of clients or meet the goals of projects and expectations within a time.

The past has seen companies be agile in their approach and the need to maintain traditional business practices has been questioned by the ever-changing nature of the tech-driven business environment.

While the conventional methods aren't fast enough, but their complexity and complexity to deal the new challenges is minimal. But, companies must be able to meet the demands of their customers.

Therefore, these issues and the necessity of addressing the demands of these times have led to experts in technology, focusing on managing projects, managing products and software development. They are able to develop Agile software, a revolutionary model of software development and a new way of working. Differently.

Responsiveness requirements have forced from the shadows and inaccessibility of more flexible and effective tools that will not just enhance the old Waterfall methods but also and perhaps more importantly, surpass them in the end.

What's the purpose of Agile?

Many developers and project management fans have asked the typical question that every local will be asking when a new sheriff is introduced to the town. The most frequent question is: why is there a need for Agile in the first place, despite the wonderful features and functionality the traditional Waterfall provides? If the method I'm currently using is working flawlessly for me, why would I need to change to a different method?

However, change can be the sole thing permanent and you can be certain that each upgrade to an existing model, especially within the IT world is unpredictable. Think about the time when Windows XP, Linux and Windows 7 were in vogue as you compare the features and functions offered by Windows 8 and 10 to these. Both cycles are worlds different, and it's not a surprise.

The area of management and development of products isn't any the same. The methods of development for products that were acceptable 10 years ago is no longer able to be used to achieve the dynamism that technological advancements have created.

What you considered to be first-rate yesterday isn't going to be able to pass the test of today. What's "fast enough" will not be sufficient for tomorrow's requirements and ever-changing demands.

The most significant benefit of Agile technology is that it puts businesses at a competitive advantage that allows them to use Agile methods to help them keep up with the rapid pace of technological advancement.

Through the Agile method software companies are able to develop software faster and with lower cost than is available using Waterfall. Thus, Agile gives software developers an advantage in a highly competitive market. It sounds like a theoretical and abstract. Okay, let's discuss the advantages of Agile in terms that are concrete.

As an upgrade to Waterfall, Agile does not need a lot of planning nor extensive planning during the initial phase of an initiative. Every stage of the project, Agile practices and methodologies can be modified in response to feedback from customers.

Agile can be considered as a familiar procedure, which is smaller waterfalls which have extremely quick iterations, and a high speed of response. Teams that are agile are multi- and multi-functional, and are able to create several iterations of a project at several weeks at a period of.

With Agile software, you can to arrange all tasks delivered into an agenda. Iterations of work are defined in relation to values of work in relation to the requirements and goals of both the business and the customer. After each iteration the final product remains a still in the process of being developed.

But, prioritizing needs and projects, as also coordinating the needs of business and customers is a crucial task that both developers and business people must work out.

Afquainting yourself with Agile Practice

So, what exactly is Agile? Simply put, Agile is the process of developing software. It is an iterative, incremental method of development of software.

In the context of a process, Agile is used to describe a way of managing projects as well as an overall way of thinking about software development. It is interesting to note that Agile development has its roots and application in the field of technology more than in the sciences. Also, the process is more grounded in reality, rather than in academia.

Agile methods and practices can be used in the development of software and across all areas of an organization's life. This is the reason why the leadership of Agile methods promotes teamwork, close customer collaboration, frequent and quick delivery of tools and work and tools, clear communication, accountability, and the capability to react to change.

Agile was initially designed to make it easier for change agile process manager as well as software engineers. Therefore, using Agile industry managers as well as IT experts can react to the changing demands and trends by releasing required capabilities.

Additionally, in the process of creating an Agile framework and turning it into an effective model over Waterfall is the requirement to answer a range of questions that companies and software developers are trying for answers to. These questions may include:

* What are the most important things that good Agile team members and practitioners be aware of and do?

How can we help teams and developers to be good users of Agile?

* How do we make the transition from planning-driven Waterfall development to Agile development that is practice-focused?

What tools are available are available to help you practice Agile development?

* How can these tools employed to support Agile practices?

What can businesses and organizations manage their projects by using different Agile frameworks and practices?

* How can organizations as well as organizational processes and industries develop an efficiency model that will assist in the achievement of team-focused instead of individual-oriented collaboration?

How can industries define their job responsibilities according to the client's goals?

* Why should software companies identify their work as designers, analysts testers, programmers as well as project management?

The benefits of agile Processes

Allows for flexible change

When the focus is on value, the process of change is an investment for processes. Agile processes allow for real change during iteration. Items on the Product Backlog may be modified and prioritized to satisfy the requirement for urgent needs. The team is more in control over the management and customization of the Product Backlog, reviewing procedures and track the progress of projects. The work must be delivered early to ensure the anticipated Return on Investment.

Costs that can be predicted and schedule

Its fixed structure of each Sprint provides the team with the sense of security in terms of costs and schedule, as well as the result of the work completed. The team is able mix estimated costs prior to every Sprint providing the client with an idea of what it would cost to have their task completed with the help of the team. This way it is easy and better decision-making and prioritizing the work of the team as well as the client.

It allows Transparency

The agile methodology actively involves the client right from beginning to the end. The process involves the client at the first sound of the whistle during the plan stage, by way of review sessions until the time a new feature is integrated into the software. Clients can view and track the progress of a project throughout its phases, but not until the conclusion that the work is completed. This is a way to encourage transparency and involvement of all parties.

The focus is on value

Agile offers the platform that allows the team to concentrate on the value their software can bring to the table. They are focused on answering questionslike: What is the customer's want? What can we do to help the company expand? What software can we use to offer features that provide the greatest value to our client's business?

User-focused

Agile processes are used to define specifications and features as they assist in promoting business growth and acceptance by utilizing the stories of users. Concentrating on the user's requirements and expectations enables the team deliver the best value, not just an IT project that is geared towards consumers.

In each step, Agile processes allow consumers and users to review and give feedback to team and the developers by tests after each Sprint.

Enhances Quality

Agile allows projects to be split into smaller units to alleviate the burden of heavy work to the entire team. The aim is to increase efficiency and speed of development. This way testing of projects and team cooperation become seamless. When teams are split into smaller groups who focus on distinct aspects of the project, results are more thorough. In this way, as well conducting tests reviews through the process, any defects or mistakes can be quickly identified and rectified.

It defines the purpose of your team

Agile methods are based on creating value and a shared sense of responsibility and goals for everyone on the team. Simply put, every participant in your team has the right to be the owner of the task. This is because it provides your team with an identity and purpose instead of creating an illusion of urgency. It is interesting to note that teams with a purpose have more success and are more efficient and productive than a group of people without synergy.

Chapter 2: Augmentative Manifesto

Each and every project is guided by the values of a certain set of fundamentals as well as short, medium and long-term plans. These values are the principles that be the basis for the actions and duties of the creators and innovators of ideas and designs in all fields.

The authors from the Agile project are also of the opinion that there are certain ethical rules that must guide the work and activities for software engineers. By embracing these values, software developers build trust with their the team and customers, as well as confidence and confidence in themselves.

What is the Agile The Agile Manifesto?

Agile The Manifesto thus refers to an agreement that outlines the four fundamental values and 12 principles that software developers can apply to improve their skills and provide high-quality IT services for clients.

The idea is that the proper management and the maintenance of a great relationships with clients is more than having the necessary skills and experience. Agile authors believe that it's not only enough to get the standard IT agreements. Best practices effectively assist software developers to maximize the quality of service, particularly in a market in which there are many service providers within the IT sector.

The manifesto outlines four core values as well as 12 fundamentals. Each of the sections gives software developers new insights into decentralizing the complex processes that define software development.

The goal of the Manifesto

The purpose for the declaration, besides other goals, is to transform the whole process of developing software. The processes of developing software over decades have been burdened by many bureaucratic processes. These processes, too, are inflexible and uni-dimensional regards to documentation requirements.

The four values that are outlined within the Agile Manifesto are designed to foster a an approach to software development which is focused on quality by the creation of products that satisfy the expectations and needs of the consumer.

The same way the 12 principles are designed to create and support the development of software that is geared towards the needs of the client. The principles will provide an environment that aligns with the business's plans and strategies, none less quickly responding to feedbacks and changes from the viewpoint of the user.

The manifesto aims to keep the balance and bring credibility back to the methodology's claims. The purpose of Agile manifesto, as the authors say, will be not just to plan, but also to recognize the limits of planning in a constantly changing digital world.

In addition, the authors insist on a method of software development which is based on the idea of developing software gradually. This approach is to allow Agile users with updates to versions or updates of software, in brief sprints.

Four principles of Agile Manifesto

The Agile Manifesto affirms the four key values that define Agile Software Development. These include:

* Interactions between individuals and processes and tools

* Working software over comprehensive documentation;

* Customer collaboration on contract negotiation

• Collaboration with customers over contract negotiation

* Reacting to changes according to the plan.

The 12 principles of the Agile Manifesto

The 12 principles set out in the Agile The Agile Manifesto are:

1. Customer Satisfaction

The Agile methods are developed to meet the requirements and requirements of customers by rapid and consistent production of high-quality work. It is believed that software developers will only gain trust from clients through timely and dependable prioritization of their requirements.

2. Keeping sizeable workload

The Agile methodologies focus on breaking big projects down into manageable parts that can be completed in a short time. The key word is simplicity. the Agile manifesto.

Fundamentally the majority of Agile methodologies are based on the concept of maximizing the amount work not being done. They are relentlessly focused on minimizing functions that do not add value to the process of chin.

3. Self-organized team

Agile recognizes that delivering the finest designs, works, and architectures and delivery needs that the team is organized. But, a team can not become organized from scratch and must be self-motivated and self-organize to produce the most effective solution.

Through this process self-organized teams become multi-functional and cross-functional. It can identify risks and issues with the project even before they become serious obstacles in the course of the undertaking.

4. Accepting Change Requirements

Software developers are more effective and responsive to customer requirements only when they realize the importance of embracing change, even at the end of phases of development that are part of the process. Agile methodologies and processes are designed in that they are able to accommodate the changing demands.

The changes, however, must be used to enhance the competitive advantage. The Agile project is a way to avoid despair when faced with changes, no matter how difficult changes in requirements can appear to the project manager or developer.

Responding to changes as quickly and efficiently as is possible will allow the developer in achieving the clients' needs. It can be a great indicator of advancement.

5. Sustainable Effort

The creation of processes that help sustain efforts and collective growth is crucial for creating a harmonious work environment. agile processes and methodologies recognize and support that initiative.

Ideally, Agile is designed in the way that it ensures that each member of the chain of process- developers, sponsors and usersshould be able to operate at a the same pace and keep that for a long time.

The motto "think, work, and balance' is a good fit in the concept of a sustainable endeavor. Everyone must be actively engaged in the process of getting the project to its end phase. So it will be a high-quality work performed to the same manner that the team also gets positively impacted.

Agile is determined to ensure the same amount of activity between participants in the chain process. This will result in greater capacity to predict.

6. Progress measurement

How do you measure progress based on the quantity of work completed? This is one of the key aspects of Agile methods. The development of software is among the main factors used to gauge the progress of work.

The goal's objective should be more important than the strict adhering to a plans. This is since the greater your involvement are in executing plans the more distracted you are from the main purpose of the venture.

Agile emphasizes the need for constant document updates which is not a result of tracking progress, but a strict adherance to the plans.

7. Update-driven and value-added solution

When it comes to Agile is involved, technical expertise and well-designed designs improve agility. This is why it is essential to pay attention on this part of your project.

The result that is derived from a stunning design is much more effective and valuable than a sleek design. It will give you an outcome that can endure the test of time.

Agile processes also believe that the best thing about Agile processes is the answer that is flexible and able to continuous updates that keep it within the loop of currency.

A beautiful design in Agile assessment, should not only be a solution provider, but and more importantly , provides an option that will keep its value by updating as well as maintenance.

8. Rapid and frequent project delivery

Agile methods are based on the idea of delivering regularly. The notion is that frequent delivery of software that is working helps developers get faster feedback from the end users. Developers will then be able quickly determine the areas that need to be modified.

The quicker a developer is able to deliver incremental software and the faster it is delivered, the better for the entire team. The preference for a shorter timeframe is essential to identify an unintentional error when developing or communicating with clients.

It is better to use an Agile method to discover early where the error is and fix it quickly rather instead of having to complete the job to be done in rework.

9. The project is being worked through

Software developers and project managers should collaborate to complete the project throughout the whole process. Additionally, it's appropriate to allow the customer to be a part of the delivery process.

The process of working through the project is in recognizing that both the client and the developer work towards the same objective.

10. Direct Conversation

The use of face-to-face to facilitate communicating between members of the team is as important as the main objective of the group. Teams perform the best and efficiently if they can learn the process of communicating information face-to face.

While sharing a area is a good idea and even encouraged but having an osmotic form of communication, where co-location is not possible, could be effective in delivering the same results when handled correctly.

The team leaders need to ensure that everyone is aware of progress through directly communicating. Utilizing a third party to communicate messages could hinder the whole process and hinder the goals that the entire team. It is therefore essential to improve the technical side of communication methods among the team.

11. Motivational Team Members

The members of a team are eager to create projects. They would like to be part of a team people who are trusted to work on projects. Project managers and developers have to motivate team members by offering them an great working conditions that support them.

Agile methodologies and processes emphasize self-organizing teams that spontaneously and uninhibited are able to handle them and their work. The need for micromanagement of projects might not be needed anymore.

12. Utilize After Action Review for Effectiveness

The concept of reflection is one that aspect that the Agile manifesto lists as a key principle that results in amazing results and boosts team synergy. Each week the team members need to meet to discuss how they can be more effective.

It's in the process that they can introduce fresh ideas, adjust and fine tune the behavior of members. Utilizing After-Action Review helps you improve on the next project you are working on for clients to come back. It is also important to look back at projects that have been completed to ensure you deliver an improved version to come up with a better one in the near future.

Agile projects are characterized by a number of ceremonies, one of which is the Retrospective. After each Sprint or Iteration Agile suggests that teams gather to discuss and rectify any shortcomings prior to starting an entirely new project.

Failure to conduct a review could result in a serious risk and can have a negative effect on your project. Because agile is built on transparency and technical excellence respect, trust, and dedication, forming efficient teams will help to value the individual and their interactions over processes as well as tools.

Chapter 3: Agile Methodologies

Agile methodologies refer to various methods and models within which the Agile method can be applied. The kind of methodology to be employed is determined by the task that the team wishes to tackle.

There are many different methodologies used to implement the Agile process. Although they draw their design and methodology from one Agile source, the methods differs in how they are executed. This includes:

1. Extreme programming

This is among the methods employed for implementing Agile practice. It is an application of project management and software development approach that is designed to increase efficiency and adaptability to changes and evolving demands.

It is also a reference to the agile development approach which is used in software development that allows programmers and developers to determine the delivery scope.

Extreme Programming (XP) remains one of the most well-known however, it is also a controversial and contested agile framework. If you are a software developer looking to consistently and rapidly deliver high-quality software and consistency, this controlled method is the most suitable option to employ.

One of the features it one of its strengths is that Extreme Programming encourages customer participation and everyone is a part of the tightly knit team right beginning at the planning phase.

Extreme Programming is a method of programming. Extreme Programming operates on four fundamental principles:

1. Simplicity

2. Communication

3. Feedback

4. Courage

Beyond these fundamentals The framework also includes 12 practices for backup:

1. Make a game plan

2. Releases should be made in smaller steps

3. Conduct customer acceptance tests

4. Make design simple

5. Perform programming in pairs

6. The development process should be driven through tests

7. It's a feature that keeps coming back

8. Integrate continuously

9. Code ownership by the team

10. Create standards for the coding

11. Representation

12. Keep workable working speed

2. Kanban

Kanban is a framework that is based in the spirit of visualization of Agile. It's a method for managing work, with an focus on just-in time delivery. In conjunction with the Kanban system are Kanban Board. Kanban Board.

The Kanban board is visualisation of workflow and work device that gives a clear overview of the current status, progress and any issues associated with the work. This kind of flexible execution is a great way to make small, continuous modifications to the system.

Kanban framework works by following tenets:

* Visual workflow

* Restricting work-in-progress

* Improvement as well as management of the workflow

* Clearly stating the policies

* Continuous improvement

Kanban Four Principles of Operation

Kanban is based on four fundamental principles:

1. There is no setup, there is no procedure

This sounds like fresh! It's exactly that what Kanban is. As with many aspects of an Agile projects, Kanban does not have any predefined set of parameters or an order of operation. It allows teams to get started the present; however, you are able to add Kanban features over workflows you already have. This way you can introduce changes.

2. Be relentless with incremental, rather than sweeping changes

Kanban is a system that is in line with gradual, evolutionary changes. Because the framework is built to face minimal resistance and encourages constant incremental and evolutionary modifications to the current system. The framework doesn't encourage drastic changes because of its resistance capability.

3. Concentrate on the existing process and its role

The Kanban design recognizes that existing roles, processes and responsibilities are valuable within themselves. Therefore, Kanban doesn't prohibit process but it doesn't mandate either. A process that is in place can produce the desired outcomes and also provide acceptance to the Kanban implementation. A sudden change in process can alter the configuration and speed.

4. The leadership qualities must be displayed at all levels

This isn't an exclusive operational process of the Kanban method. A variety of Agile methods, such as Scrum, RAD also adopt the principle. It doesn't matter to which section of the ladder you are on, you must be a leader.

In other words it's not necessary become a member of the team member or an executive to play the leading job. If you are a frontline member of for any team, you're required to exhibit that character. Be sure to exhibit character that encourages team spirit and an attitude that promotes continuous development to meet the team's goal.

In contrast Kanban against Scrum Models

Kanban has a few indistinguishable similarities in common with Scrum framework. But, the two frameworks have some distinct differences that must not be confused with one another.

Scrum Kanban

Cadence Regularly scheduled sprints of fixed length (that is, two months) Continuous flow

Method of Release at the end of every sprint, it is determined whether the owner of the product accepts continuous delivery or at the discretion of the team

Roles Scrum master, Product Owner Scrum development team, scrum master None currently exist. Some teams seek the assistance from an agile coach

Key metrics include Velocity Cycle time.

Change process Teams must strive not to make any changes to the sprint plan in the course of the course of the sprint. Any changes could affect learnings . Changes could occur anytime during the sprint.

3. Rapid Application Development (RAD)

This is an Agile Methodology for Development that allows software developers and programmers to develop solutions at the speed light through direct communication with the end-users to satisfy business needs.

In simple words, RAD is less talk and more action since it doesn't emphasize the importance of rigid planning. While the approach emphasizes the importance of action over planning, RAD demands that the developer follow certain steps during the process of development. The steps that must be followed are to identify requirements, design prototypes, solicit feedback from users and build more prototypes, then try, and then implement.

RAD is popular for your team, particularly when you must finish a project quickly. It can deliver a functional system faster than the traditional method like Waterfall will accomplish. Make use of RAD only when you have the funds. It is because it requires an entire team of highly skilled and experienced developers. They will require some cool money. Thirdly, you could use rapid application development if you have a client and user pool who are able to test your prototypes.

Why do we use RAD?

The benefits of the use of RAD for the development of your application is the fact that you can build a functional product quicker. This means that you can showcase your work-in-progress in a piecemeal fashion, permitting your team to put it together at the end of the process.

Additionally, it allows you to receive direct and constant feedback from your user. As you are able to display to your client or user the work you are working on and they will send you what you must take out, change or modify. You can receive their feedback as quickly and directly as you'd like. This gives you the chance to make improvements on your work, and making implementation more simple.

Additionally, using RAD provides you with the flexibility to break up a big project into smaller pieces and projects. There are two possibilities that RAD offers. Oneis that when you're creating a big app, breaking the application down into smaller units will allow you to create more of a specialized team of developers that focus on a specific section in the work. The other benefit comes from the previous one: it is possible to create small successes for your team members, allowing you to inspire the team to work harder. That way, you will have more hands-on experience to guide them throughout the entire process.

4. Lean Software Development

The Lean Software Development process is among the Agile iteration techniques. It was first created by Mary and Tom Poppendieck. Learn is an established set principles that can be applied to the development of software in order to lessen the burden on costs programming, mismatches, and defects. The approach focuses on creating value and offering the clients a value-driven and efficient process to their software project.

Seven fundamentals of the Lean Framework

* Waste Removal

* Amplify Learning

* Decision-making that is late

* Rapid result delivery

* Help the team.

* Build Integrity

Intuitively envision the entire application

The benefits of Lean Framework Lean Framework

1. Lean eliminates roadblocks

Within the framework of Learn software development, the term "waste" is things that are capable to reduce the quality of code or hampering the time and effort used in the process of programming. It can also be described as any roadblock that hinders the delivery of business value. Examples of bottlenecks could include ineffective code or functions delay in programming, unclear requirements, or insufficient testing.

2. Customer needs are met at a lower cost

The primary goal of the Lean method is to get rid of these barriers by implementing the appropriate technology and understanding what the customer actually wants and wants. Another benefit of the Lean framework is that clients can take a decisions in the late hours, but with knowledge, and thus reduce the amount they spend in the project.

3. Increases the value of your business

As an iterative framework for development, Lean is poised to create new applications and enhancements efficiently and in a cost-effective method. This is why the integrity of the framework is built-in to ensure an uninterrupted flow of architecture and system components.

4. It is easy to incorporate

Lean principle gives companies the power to integrate and continue to improve when they swiftly introduce and make changes to their systems.

5. Crystal

Crystal Agile framework is one method for the creation of software that is light and flexible. As a method, Crystal features several agile methods, including Clear, Crystal Yellow, Crystal Orange, and other distinct methods associated with Agile.

There are many elements that influence Crystal processes, such as how large the group is, significance to the process, as well as the goals of the project that the team is working on. Crystal methods operate on the idea that every project is distinct in its own way. In the same way, the guidelines and procedures that will govern their implementation must be tailored to the particular requirements and features in order in order to meet the needs of the client.

Crystal is, as do the majority of the Agile methods, also operates by its own unique tenets, principles and principles. Alongside these principles, Crystal focuses on promoting regular and timely releases of software. In addition this, the Agile method also promotes the highest level of user engagement, increases the ability to adapt and removes distractions, as well as the enforcing of bureaucracy.

The crystal principles are:

* Teamwork

* Communication

* Simplicity

* Reflection

* Frequent adjustments

* Processes that are improved

Chapter 4: Sprint And Sprint Cycle

What exactly is Sprint?

Scrum sprint is a phrase commonly used for Agile methodology. It is a time-boxed cycle of scrum development. In a sprint, a team designs, plans and determines how much work they want to finish and then prepares to be reviewed. In a brief, common sense particularly for athletics Sprint can refer to a brief race that's run at a full speed.

Development Teams decide on a shorter time frame for the term "sprint", which is usually between 2 and four weeks. Scrum Sprint requires that the team sets together the goals (technically known as Sprint Goal) they want to achieve and is carried out in conjunction and with the Product Owner. This work program is listed by priority order within the Sprint backlog at the time of Sprint Planning session.

After the team has started Scrum sprints, the the team collaborates to finish the planned work in a timely manner and have it available for review by the Product Manager, Scrum Master, stakeholders and customers as well as other stakeholders at the end of the time.

Prior to beginning the Sprint cycle, the team is required and must have read the high-level User Stories in the Product backlog. With the aid by Sprint Analytics, Scrum Master and Product Owners can track the progress of teamwork during a Sprint at a single glance. The Sprint Analytics assists team members from the Development Team, Scrum Master and product Owner define a Sprint Goal and evaluate the work that is completed within each Sprint.

The following figure provides an outline of Scrum Flow for one Sprint:

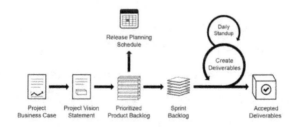

Sprint Cycle

Every Sprint begins with an Sprint Planning Meeting. This is the time when together that the team will decide to include top priority User Stories in the Sprint. In general, a Sprint is not longer than one to six weeks. During this time members of the Scrum Team works on generating potential shippable Deliverables, or product increments.

When the Sprint is in progress The team (which comprises The Product Owner, Scrum Master, Development Team and the stakeholders) also hold daily, short, and highly focused Standup Meetings. These are the meetings where team members debate their daily the progress made.

In the final phase of the Sprint the team will conduct the Sprint Review as a way to engage stakeholders. In the time of this Review team members from the Scrum Development Team provides demonstrable outputs from the project they've been working on to the Product Owner as well as those who are involved in the project.

The objective for review Review is to get their opinions and comments about the project. The Product Owner approves the Deliverables only when they meet the established Acceptance Criteria and Specifications for the Project. The proposal is rejected, and the group is then asked to revise the project in order to satisfy the expectations.

Following the Review After the Review, after the Review, Development Team conducts what is known as"the Sprint Retrospect Meeting where members discuss ways to improve their processes and performance to produce a more value that they can show to the rest of the team during the following Sprint Review.

Are there any differences in Sprint Iteration and Iteration?

This is a question that most newcomers to the Agile process frequently ask. Particularly with the evolving technological trends and advancements mobile and web application developers are finding it difficult and sometimes challenging to adjust the changes and advances. Another similarity are Sprint just another word for Iteration? Are we able to be able to have Sprints in Iterations, or within Sprints? How do we release interim data for clients before the scheduled Sprint release date?

An iteration is an broad term used by agile professionals to describe one development cycle. It is frequently employed in the IID which means iterative and Incremental Development. Scrum is, in contrast is an agile specialized framework or a specific Incremental Development process which uses the term Sprint to symbolize its the iterations. Also, the development cycle of Scrum is known as the Sprint.

Every Agile method is accompanied by a name that describes its variations. This means that Sprint has a name that is Scrum specific. Sprint involves an repetition. However, an iteration of Extreme programming, or Crystal or EED and so on aren't Sprints.

Chapter 5: What Is Scrum?

Learning about Scrum

Are you looking to create a dynamic team that is cross-functional and able to make everyone in your team to work towards achieving a the goal you have set, then Scrum is the ideal choice for you. Scrum was not created to concentrate on a single members of a team.

Instead, it is focused upon the group and ways they can maximize their capabilities to achieve a the goal. Similar to Jakes and his company encouraging people to work together in order to accomplish tasks more quickly and efficient manner is the best way to move.

Scrum is simply defined as the efficient and agile method of managing and executing the project, particularly software development. as one of the method improvement strategies of agile (we will talk about agile shortly) and development, rather than a methodological approach, Scrum is better viewed as a framework to manage processes. Scrum is a concept that was invented, an approach to teamwork that work together and synergizes.

Scrum is an incremental and iterative framework that is useful in managing the development of products. Scrum provides a flexible and complete product development process where the development team collaborates closely and in a team to reach a common goal.

The framework lets teams to self-organize through physical co-location, or synergizing knitted online collaboration between everyone on the team, as well as regular face-to face interaction between everyone involved in the team.

This fascinating, informative and thought-provoking book sets the stage for the management and leadership process across a variety of sectors. It is altering not just how we interact with colleagues, but also our lives and our thinking process.

It was evident from our tragic story that the primary focus of Jakes and his staff, throughout the years, must not be on hiring, firing or headhunting. The energy should have been directed toward helping the top management and upper levels combine their diverse abilities and knowledge to bear on the company.

Scrum and Agile Differentialities and similarities

A term that is closely linked to Scrum refers to Agile. We've covered this extensively in our very first chapter but it is essential to look at it in comparison to Scrum and one of its 'offspring'. In the end you will recognize agile as the term used to describe the broad range of all approaches and methods which bring about changes within your Development Team' process.

Let's look at the connection with Scrum and agile as follows The kitchen's Dishwasher was damaged by its high energy usage and you have to replace it. You visit an electronic retailer where you can browse through a variety of models and brands of TVs.

You will see Samsung, Panasonic, Frigidaire, LG, Hisense, Tecno, Bosch and so on. In the end, you decide to go with and leave with, say, Bosch. Bosch possibly because you believe it is resistant towards high voltage. This is exactly how Scrum connects to agile. Imagine agile as a dishwasher, whereas Scrum is the favorite Bosch Scrum, which is one of the brands of dishwashers.

However, here's the difference that you might not be able customize your dishwasher but agile processes, such as Scrum can be adapted to fit your needs. In that scenario you could incorporate additional desirable features you see in other agile methods into Scrum.

You could, for instance, make use of elements that are part of Extreme programming, for instance test-driven development or pairing programming into Scrum processes. This is the type of flexibility and personalization that is offered by agile. The flexibility offered by the agile method is one of the characteristics that are appealing to its many users.

Scrum is one of numerous agile methods that contain other agile processes like Extreme Programming, Adaptive System Development, DSDM, Feature Driven Development, Kanban, Crystal and many more.

Agile is a term that refers to change and is a generic term that covers all the activities and methodologies in software development. It is used to describe a broad approach to the goal of software development. Every one of the agile methodologies that are used, such as Scrum is focused on:

1. Teamwork

2. The frequent delivery of software that works

3. Close collaboration with customers

4. Ability to react quickly to any change.

One key benefits of agile methods is the fact that they break down an entire software project into smaller, manageable pieces. This allows developers to manage projects in small increments and iterations.

This is what makes the Agile management method from other management approaches. Agile, similar to Scrum management, makes use of iterations throughout the process of development of software.

Agile methods are based on research-based results that have proven that a the larger portion of work does not always yield the expected results. Furthermore, studies have proven that the less time a project takes is, the greater its success rate.

The goal of agile development is to minimize as much as is possible the size of the project so that it can create as many smaller projects as is possible. This helps teams manage and complete the iteration quickly.

Benefits of Scrum Methodology

While it might be difficult to make the switch from, say Crystal and DSDM or other agile approach it's a breeze by using Scrum. The adoption of the Scrum procedure has positive feedbacks which appear to set it apart from other agile methodologies. The advantages from using the Scrum framework are interconnected and are built into one another. These comprise:

* Greater productivity

* Higher quality

* Shorter time-to-market

* Improved stakeholder satisfaction

* Greater job satisfaction

Engaged employees

Chapter 6: Anatomy Of The Scrum

What should you be looking for in Scrum Features?

The Scrum framework is comprised of many parts that all leaders must keep an eye on. Each element is crucial to the totality of the system for organization's development and process improvement. Additionally, each module is part of the framework for specific functions and purposes to ensure the general applicability and use that the framework provides.

It is the Scrum Framework is the combination of what's known as Scrum Teams. Teams are comprised of members roles as well as events, artifacts and rules. In the end, the rules act as the bridge which connect the events, roles, and artifacts. The rules act as rules, but if broken, they could result in disruption of processes and inefficient operation, and utilization of the whole system, as well as impacting the those who are part of it. We will now look at the various components.

Scrum Rules

Here are some rules that will that will save you time in time, money and resources. The Scrum framework is composed of often-repeated rules that govern the application and application of this framework. As mentioned earlier that the rules act as bridges that tie the various constituents of the framework. The rules hold the Scrum process so that everyone can participate and follow.

Remove the foundation and the whole structure collapses. take away the bridge the interconnectivity and communication stop and chaos ensues. If you know the purpose and meaning behind chain action, you know the vital role of the rules are throughout the Scrum blueprints.

Here's the most exciting news item that could inspire leaders to embrace this Scrum framework.

There is no reason for management to not take the initiative to adopt the framework. In addition, the Scrum system includes its own Scrum Master which helps in making sure that everyone in the team is following the rules of Scrum in relation to the specific project.

The principal purpose behind Scrum guidelines is to increase efficiency. The rules are formulated in the framework to facilitate the improvement of processes, improve the development system, reduce waste, and efficiently make the most of limited energy and resource. Below is a list fundamental rules of Scrum: Scrum model:

1. Each Sprint is Four Weeks or less in duration.

2. There aren't any breaks in between Sprints

3. The Same Length of Every Sprint is the same length

4. The purpose of every Sprint is "Potentially transportable" Software

5. Each Sprint contains Sprint Planning

6. Sprint Planning Meeting Sprint Planning Meeting is Time set to 2 hours / Week of Sprint Duration

7. The Daily Scrum happens each day at the same time.

8. It is the Daily Scrum is time boxed to 15 minutes.

9. Each Sprint comes with a Sprint review to solicit feedback from stakeholder about the product

10. Each Sprint includes a Sprint Retrospectives to allow the team to review and adjust

11. The Review as well as Retrospective Meetings are time recorded in total up to 2 hours per week in Sprint length

12. There isn't a break in Between Sprint Review and Retrospective meetings

Scrum Rules against the Generally Accepted Scrum Practice (Non-Core Scrum Rules)

Be careful not to misinterpret Scrum rules with Scrum guidelines with the what might be thought of as the generally accepted Scrum Practices which is abbreviated as GASP. This could also be regarded in the context of Non-Core Scrum Rules (NCSR).

While the Scrum rule is a legally binding process that , if the team doesn't follow it, they're not doing Scrum A GASP is an activity that a enough Scrum teams are engaged in. We will present it shortly in the form of a table. This will help us when working with the framework.

However, we must first define in a formal way what we are referring to by GASP as well as NCSR. Here's an example of a definition that we can follow.

In addition, holding the review meeting of the sprint at the conclusion of the sprint may be a GASP, or NCSR and is not an actual Scrum norm. But, a tea can still be considered conducting scrum even though they don't attend the sprint review meeting. There are teams that enjoy in common practice, an after-sprint mini-review rather than participating in a formal and larger sprint review.

For example, in an engineering team working on software, members could decide to hold brief reviews of their intervals with their product manager at the end of each iteration. Following this review is completed, team members could release the new feature on the website right away.

Or, the team could at the conclusion of the project decide to conduct a review of the project. In that the team conducts every sprint review one at a time, at the end of each cycle. No matter what method they choose to use the process will still be based on Scrum.

What exactly is GASP and NCSR?

The Generally Accepted Scrum Practices (GASP) also known as the non-core Scrum Guidelines (NCSR) are an array of activities that are carried out by a huge amount, but it is not necessary that every Scrum teams. In the meantime, a team that is not performing any of the activities would remain carrying out Scrum.

Teams' activities that take the form of shorter Iterations that are time-boxed rather than an entire calendar month aren't considered to be GASP. It is more of an exception to the Scrum norm because, generally, Scrum encourages time-boxing rather than an hourly estimation.

Therefore, for any practice to qualify as GASP, it should be widely considered to be an excellent idea. This is what defines GASP as meaning the following "every Scrum team should be aware of being not part of the process.

However, their absence from the team isn't a sign that they are not exempt. In fact, they may choose to participate in other methods that are not in line with what other Scrum teams are doing.

Chapter 7: User Shows, And Cadence

A user story is short, concise description of a feature. It is typically written by or from the viewpoint of the user or user. It could also be a concise description of a requirement for a product or a business scenario for the customer that is narrated by a product manager.

The user's story can be written by the user themselves or by the team comprising the product's owner, the members of the development team and Scrum Master. The story should be written in a simple way to assist the readers understand the capabilities that the program has.

The person who wants the capability is often writing an evaluation of the way the system operates. Users of the system are typically advised to share their experiences with the systems they utilize instead of listing their capabilities. User stories are typically written on sticky notes, and then stored in a shoe box. They can also be arranged on tables or on walls to help facilitate discussions.

The telling of a user's story usually follows a certain pattern, such as:

"As an individual user (you are able to mention the category of user you belong to)I'd like/can (state the purpose of the desired product)/so it can (give reasons to stop using this products)."

Example of User Storiesfrom Users:

* As a driver I would like to be able accept credit card payments to allow my passengers to pay in a seamless manner.

* As a rider I would like to join My Master Card to my account so that I can make payments without cash or

As a driver, I'd like put up my profile picture and the one of my vehicle to attract more people.

As a driver I'd like to see all the possible vehicles to pick one from the pool that I am comfortable with.

Who wrote user stories?

This is a crucial issue that has a straightforward answer anyone is able to write user stories. The first step is to ensure that the product owner ensures that he develops a Product Backlog that is Agile User Stories.

But, writing the User Story proper requires all hands on deck. There is a belief in some circles that the user is the only person who is writing a User Story. This is not true. Anyone on the team, such as Team Leader, Product Owner Team, Scrum Master or even external members such as the users who are stakeholders can write these.

Every team member on any Agile project of course must include user stories written by them. The way that stories are created is more important than the person who is writing the story.

Tips for writing great User Stories

It's not enough to write or create an User Story. It is an essential part of your team's work. Apart from being aware that you have to structure the story of the user in such as to ensure that it's at all times written in the user's perspective You must follow the following guidelines to assist you in writing a great User Story. This will help you save lots of time talking about what needs to be constructed.

Here are some trusted tips for creating an User Story:

1. Create a story from the Users Side

Like the title suggests that a user story is the details of how a software product can impact the customer. The story is either told by the person using the product or by the team, a customer story should write from the viewpoint of the software user or the consumer. Another way to think about it is that the user story describes the way a consumer utilizes or uses a product. Whatever the case the product should have an its impact on the final outcome of the customer and the tale must be told from the perspective of the user. Furthermore the stories of users must be targeted to highlight the specific features of the product.

2. Make a story. Don't perform a task.

A story isn't an identical task. When writing or telling a user story, it has to express feelings and provide feedback. The user story needs a variety of tasks to achieve the desired outcomes and have the necessary impact. This is because the task is all with implementation, while the user story is all about the what it means. User stories must convey the "what" about an item, not the what.'

3. Keep it simple, but remain top-of-the-line

Being 'high-level' does not suggest that your story is a separate one from the rest of your target audience. No. It is essential to be precise and direct to the point. The user stories need to be written in a plan straightforward and solid language.

It will also aid the team and other stakeholders to recognize the expectations and needs from the end user. Therefore, it can help users avoid spending too much time explaining complex concepts, buzzwords and abbreviations.

4. Learn to recognize the needs of users

It is essential to keep up-to-date with the latest trends and needs of consumers. This will allow you to find out and understand the people who actually use your products are. Then, you'll be able to discover their preferences, understand their profiles and points perspective, and find the pain points that they experience by using the software. Studying user requirements as well as other methods could provide insight into an understanding of most important and actual users.

5. Utilize epic stories

When you write User stories, one factor to consider is using epics. Epic user stories leave an enormous impression on the readers. There are many ways to use epics to tell your story. One method is to use the information multiple sprints, which is a large amount of work, to explain big pieces of function

In addition, because epics are used to organize stores and providing a greater perspective of impact, epics may be described by putting smaller stories to achieve an end-to-end goal.

6. Sort stories by importance, don't throw them away. them.

One of the best ways to create great user stories and impact on user stories is to constantly enrich your product's backlog with new user stories. Keep describing new scenarios for interaction with users and get concepts and incorporate out of the box activities that impact your product.

A successful prioritization procedure also requires the proper classification of new entries. It can help to reduce the risk of chaos. Don't remove or filter objects from your archive.

7. Make sure you are prepared for success and not just acceptance

One aspect that scrum teams do not consider is how a user's story can affect the acceptance of a product. Beyond the 'it's working or 'oh, that software is great feedback you typically receive from users Your user story must provide metrics that show the direct feedback of users and show the ways your product can make users feel happy and involved. Acceptance is a must to achieve a clear understanding of the development process of the feature. But, it is also a sign that the success of your product has a mid- and longer-term impact, and is beneficial to the actual customers for your solution.

8. #Tag stories

Based on the complexity of your product, it is possible to should make use of more than thousands of stories from users. When you have several user stories it is simpler for users to navigate through and communicate with them if you make use of hashtags.

To do this, you will need to identify your stories, organize, categorize, and label your stories. The most common mistake is to change or name the story's description after the first few revisions to the story. This can cause confusion for the reader and create gaps within the team due to the inconsistencies it can cause.

Be sure to properly manage the metadata of your stories - status and progress, links, priority, resources, for example. This will enable you to research your backlog, track and analyze your backlog.

The User Story Processes

A typical User Story should undergo three distinct steps before it is accepted. Each of these three elements must be absent in the User Story you create. These are the features: Card, Confirmation, and Conversation.

Card

The Card, also known as The written version of the user's Story is a kind of invitation as well as an initial announcement for a conversation. One of the underlying principles of scrum is that teams don't have to write down everything within the Product Backlog perfectly all at one time. The process of changing and modifying would happen at a later point. Therefore the Card is a declaration that both the client as well as the staff will explore new areas of business need while they work on it.

As an of the product

I'm able

So , that .

Conversation

The term "conversation" refers to the conversation that is conducted at the cost and on the initiative from the Product Manager. The discussion is open to all stakeholders as well as the team. The conversation may be recorded verbally or in writing.

The conversation is a broad spectrum of topics. Most importantly, it is the core of the actual importance of the story of the user. Discussions during the session result in some of the elements that should be covered in the user's story. So, at any moment the Card should be adjusted to reflect the results and perspective of the those involved and the group that participated in the conversation.

Confirmation

The function as a Product Owner gets more crucial in this case. The story of a user is not considered completed unless it is approved by the Product Owner. The team and the Product Owner determine whether the story is complete or appropriate for the goal that it was created to accomplish.

The assessment and subsequent confirmation must be conducted according to the currently defined concept of "done." In addition should the current acceptance criteria do not reflect"done" as defined by "done" according to the view by the Team and the Product owner, new standards need to be created and implemented to accommodate specific requirements.

However, the existing rules must be fully accepted and understood within members of the Team before they are accepted.

The INVEST criteria of User Story

In short, each User Story has to meet the criteria for INVEST that was proposed in the book by Bill Wake, INVEST. INVEST is an acronym for Indispensable, Negotiable, Valuable Estimable, Small and Testable. Each is described below:

Independent-User Stories are the smallest of pieces of work that could be told in any order. This means that a change in one User Story does not affect the other ones. The User Stories are a distinct independent piece of art.

Negotiable - There isn't a standard or fixed procedure for the best way to implement User Stories. It's up to the team to come to a consensus on the best way to implement them.

The value of each User Story has value for the end-user and therefore must be a separate piece of it to them.

Estimable - The team can easily predict the amount of time needed to finish the creation of the User Story.

Small User Stories - Each Story has to be have a size that is as small as it can be. to go through the entire sprint cycle of creating the application, programming it, and testing.

Testable - The Team should develop the criteria can be used to verify the authenticity of a User Story has been implemented correctly and is widely accepted by the user.

How do you split Agile User Stories into two parts?

In reality, you don't have to come up with new stories every day. Sometimes, you'll have to transfer a user story onto an additional line particularly when a story from a user is too long to fit in the space of a Sprint. The most efficient and effective method is to break it up so that it appears as an implied connection. Utilize words like "and" and "or" within the story's text for two to three different stories using the pieces.

There are many ways to divide a story. Some of this includes splitting it using:

* Process step, which is, interpreting every step as a whole new story

* I/O channel - each I/O channel a distinct story

* User options, making the choices into user stories

* Data range, which means that every range that is sorted by month, year or the digit, is a new story for the user.

* CRUD actions - create or read, update, and remove. This can only be used if the it is connected with business logic.

* Role/persona: every character is a story in its own.

Cadence

The term "cadence" in Agile can be defined by the amount of weeks or days which are contained in a single sprint , or release. Also, cadence is a reference to the duration of the team's development process. In recent years, the length of time needed to create an entire sprint cycle has varied from organization to organisation. The business environment has been plural, so that businesses can choose what days they will make in the cadence.

Most organizations prefer the two-week sprint cycle. The time frame a project or company chooses to use is dependent on a range of factors , such as the project's risk, its type and the degree to which essential and crucial the project.

The table below provides one example of cadence

September 2019, September

Sunday Monday Tuesday Wednesday Thursday Friday Saturday

1 2 3 4

5 6 7 8 9 10 11

12 13 14 15 16 17 18

Chapter 8: Scrum Flow

The scientific basis of scrum projects suggests that it follows a specific procedure. The entire process begins with a vision for the project. The vision is the basis for every other aspect that needs to be created. It is true that the vision may appear to be hazy from the beginning however, as the events unfold it starts to develop and becomes more clear.

The vision may be redefined time and time again in terms of market-based to terms based on systems. The flow also includes assigning roles which has the Product Owner assuming the responsibility of defining and communicating the vision to participants in the project and financiers with the goal of increasing the ROI (ROI).

Additionally the Product Owner should make sure that he develops an effective plan for following up on projects that have been prioritized within the Product Backlog. The Product Backlog consists of the list of nonfunctional and functional requirements to meet the desired vision.

The scum flows the first step is the arrangement that is the backlog for the Products. This Product Backlog is designed in a manner the items that can bring value are given the highest priority. This is followed by clear releases. The process of organizing your Product Backlog consists of contents listing, prioritizing items with value and organizing your Product Backlog, and then the planned releases.

The Product Owner is able to make modifications to the Product Backlog according to business requirements. The modifications dependent on speed of the team's ability to bring the Product Backlog into a functional.

All work on the scrum flow are completed in sprints. Sprints are comprised of 30 calendar days. Sprint is comprised consisting of Sprint Planning, Sprint Review, Daily Scrum and Sprint Retrospective.

There is a collaborative effort among The Product Owner and the Development Team when it comes to picking priority things from the Backlog. The Product Owner will inform the Team which items on the Product Backlog he desires to be completed, the Team will then inform the Product Owner what percentage of the Product Backlog item desired list is achievable and how to convert into functionality.

Scrum Process Flow

In our chapter on previous chapters we talked about Scrum ceremonies, which is the variety of events and activities that a scrum team performs prior to the conclusion of an entire sprint. What is the relationship between these events and interconnect? Which ceremony starts and which one concludes the process? In the next few minutes, we will be discussing the sequence of events that occur during the course of a sprint.

Simply simply put, Scrum process flow refers to the process of carrying out Scrum in the most efficient method that is efficient and effective. This is the procedure that follows a step-by-step process which allows teams to utilize the scrum process to get quality, efficient results which minimize risk and increase product quality.

The scrum process begins by creating a backlog of products through to the stage of refinement for our backlog that involves reviewing and revising items to include details, estimates and orders.

During the scrum procedure as well, the development team executes the refinement process while the owner of the product updates the backlog's refinement at any point. During the planning of the sprint stage, where the team establishes the sprint's goal and the plan typically responds to questions regarding

What will be delivered during the sprint time increment?

* How can the work done during this sprint be able to meet the goal of increment?

What will be the task be completed?

It is at this point to which the development team decides on what tasks are to be accomplished in a single sprint and how to complete it by informing the owner of the product and Scrum manage the backlog of product the most important items.

The daily Scrum gathering, which is run by the team responsible for development. It's designed to improve communication, eliminate endless meetings and identify bottlenecks that may cause project delays and encourage quick decision-making.

Daily scrums allow team members to keep track of actions completed since the previous meeting. Also, it provides a platform for team members to prioritize work on the backlog of the product. The pertinent questions that need to be addressed at each daily Scrum meeting are:

* What was I able to do today to help my team reach our objective?

* What should you do to today? my team achieve our goals?

Do you know of any roadblocks or bottlenecks that stop my (or my team) from achieving the goal?

Scrum tasks

Scrum assignments are the subtle elements of work necessary to complete an entire story. A typical scrum project could take the scrum team between four and five hours to finish

When working on a scrum project teams can be assigned the tasks based on their abilities and knowledge. The sprint is a way to indicate the amount of amount of time left on the task. Also, on daily basis, those who are willing to participate can keep track of the time remaining to finish the task. The sprint indicates the hours left to complete.

If the members who are working on the task are not able to complete the task by the deadline, the remaining task is divided into other tasks. In the meantime, until the task is completed the story cannot be included. It is the (complete) job that guides the creation of the story.

How do you create and add the task

Typically, a task is included in an already existing tale by using The Story form. There are particular areas on the form where tasks from scrum can be added. There is the Tasks related list as well as The Add Scrum Tasks Related Link. But, the scrum task could be added by using the planning board or The story's progress boards.

Creating Scrum Task

For creating a scrum assignment using the Add Scrum Task place within the Story Form Follow the following steps:

1. Navigate to Agile

2. Then> Stories > Open Stories

3. Find the desired story.

4. Click on the Add Scrum Tasks Related link.

5. The amount of tasks to be added or created to this dialog box. appears.

O Analysis

o Coding

o Documentation

O Testing

6. Enter OK in order to make the task list of the type you want to select from the Scrum Tasks related list.

Scrum projects created using this method aren't yet fully completed and need to be updated to be operational.

Start each task record in scrum with a brief summary of ToDo and then define the task.

7. Complete the form according to the instructions in the table of field descriptions.

8. Save your modifications.

Eight Steps to a Complete Scrum Process Flow

1. Create what is on the backlog of your product by listing all product things and specifications in order of importance. This process is executed by the Product Manager, in conjunction with the Scrum Development Team.

2. Estimate and plan the work load based on product Backlog items at The Product Backlog Refinement Meeting. This is executed in the Scrum team Development.

3. Participate in a Sprint Planning session Meeting, which is a gathering to determine the goal of the sprint that is being achieved in the current. Iteration is the duration of one Sprint that typically ranges between one and four weeks. Choose from a list User Stories to create your Sprint Backlog to be used in the following

sprint, which can assist in helping to meet the sprint's goal.

4. Completion of complete the Sprint Backlog, giving each participant in the Scrum team task assignments that are based on that Sprint Backlog.

5. Create the Daily Scrum, which is an opportunity to talk about the progress made and to make a an assessment. Each Daily Scrum is time-boxed, typically between 15 and 20 minutes. Each member of the team must meet face-to face to discuss the topic and interact with the other team members. Daily Scrums Daily Scrum always focus on the past (what the team accomplished and accomplished yesterday) and the current (what it hopes to accomplish and achieve today) and obstacles (what can hinder the team from achieving its Sprint goals) and an review (reviewing the team's Sprint burndown chart). ***[1]

6. Plan for each day an annual scrum that can be integrated, and then successfully displayed and compiled. The version should only be released

when the team supports all of it and the unit-test is completed immediately.

7. The finalization of user stories is the end of the Sprint Backlog which means the end of an Sprint. When the Sprint there is a need to organize the Sprint Review Meeting in which both the product owner and the customer are required to participate.

8. In the final phase, the Sprint Retrospective will be held following each sprint's sprint reviews at conclusion of every sprint. In the Sprint Retrospective, the team will identify by itself the elements within the sprint that failed or did not perform in the sprint, along with solutions that could be considered.

Chapter 9: Scrum Burn Down And Velocity

This Scrum Burn down Chart refers to an estimation tool that visually shows the amount of work completed and completed within a given day versus the anticipated time to complete for the latest release of the project. The aim of the scrum burndown chart is to enable teams to keep track of the progress of projects and to deliver the desired outcome in the time frame that is agreed upon and within the timeline.

Figure 2: An example of Burndown Chart

There are a variety of ways to implement your Burndown chart. It is crucial to understand that the stories within the Scrum must be burned down in only points, and they must be minimal. Furthermore, planning poker has to be utilized to estimate the amount of work and the tasks should be burnt to the point. Thirdly, the team has to ensure that tasks are burned down must be completed in hours. [2]

Velocity

The speed at which a an Scrum development is referred to as'velocity. It is a measure of the number of stories or work that the Scrum development can complete within a single sprint. In a more detailed form the term velocity can be described as an optional however, it is often an indicator of the quantity of Product Backlog which can be converted into an increment of product within the course of a Sprint by the Scrum Team. Velocity is linked to the Scrum burn down since it's a measure of how of how the Development Team within the Scrum Team is working to accomplish the goals of a project.

As the events unfold, the content of the Scrum Product Backlog will most likely change in the time frame allocated for finalization of the task. This is as new stories will be added, while existing ones from the Product Backlog may be altered or deleted, according to what the product owner wants to do. Thus, when you look at the simple Burndown Chart, the velocity of the Scrum Team and the change in the scope of work becomes impossible to distinguish (as as shown the figure 2 in this post).

Velocity measures the quantity of work a Team is able to complete during the course of a single Sprint. Velocity is the primary measurement in Scrum. It is always, and must be measured and tracked throughout the Sprint as shown in the Sprint Burn down Chart. The outcome from the calculation of velocity must be made visible to everyone on the group. So they'll be able to determine whether the changes they make add value to their performance or not.

Ideally, Team velocity oscillate from one Sprint cycle to the next and gradually increases by 10 percent according to the Burn down chart during every Sprint. It is necessary for the Team to run three sprints before they can establish their velocity accurately. The Product Owner and Team should take their time to explain this to the stakeholders as they may not be ready to demonstrate patience until three sprints are completed.

The purpose of the Velocity

Velocity is used for a variety of reasons, including:

* It assists the team receive feedback mechanisms.

By calculating the speed, teams will be able to determine whether modifications they make have an impact positive or negatively their efficiency.

* Velocity can also assist in accurate forecasting for the team on the amount of stories that can be

finished within the same Sprint. The Sprint forecasting process can be referred to as Yesterday's Weather in Scrum.

Velocity can also assist in the process of implementing the release plan.

If you know the velocity, a Product Owner is aware of the number of Sprints it will require the Team to attain a specific standard of functionality that is available to ship.

How do you calculate Velocity an event

The velocity is determined by calculating only the user stories that are complete at the end of the process. It is not allowed to measure the quantity of work that has been completed partially. One example of incomplete job is an untested code.

In the meantime, it's feasible to estimate the speed of the Scrum Team and project the outcome after running some sprints. In other words, Scrum Team has a latitude to estimate the time until all entries within the Scrum Product Backlog will be completed. It is however not recommended to calculate points based on incomplete sprint. For stories. For instance, if , for example, the speed of an Scrum Team is say, 30 story points, and the remaining work is, for instance, 155, it's easy to assign the team an approximate number of 6 Sprint before they finish all the stories on the Backlog of Product.

Question 1.

Determine the speed of the team members in this Burn down, if at the conclusion of sprint the team is capable of completing stories 1, 2 , and 4.

Note: The team completed 50percent of the story 3 40 percent of story 5, and 40% of story.

Story 1 contains 10 points

Story 2 contains 4 points

Story 3 contains 7 points

Story 4 contains 3 points

Story 5 has 8 points.

Solution 1.

The first rule of burning down a half finished story is that it doesn't count. The team only has the ability to determine the possibility of a usable product increment. Thus, the average speed for the sprint will be 17.

If, however, the team can finish all of story 3 and the 60 percent of story 5 within the following sprint, they'll increase 15 points, making that the speed of 32 points.

Question 2.

Determine the speed of a group in the stories below when the team can complete the stories 1 , 2 and 3.

Story 1 has 5 points.

Story 2 contains 4 points

Solution 2.

The speed for this sprint is 9.

The differences between the burn chart and the velocity chart. down chart

Figure 3b:

In the the chart above the blue line shows the ideal pace for the sprint from beginning to finish, while the red line is what the actual progress that the scrum team achieved during the race.

Team progress is just beneath the blue lines indicates an area where team activity exceeded the ideal slope since team members had to complete higher number of stories than expected. The upward slope indicates the introduction of more stories, which result in additional points. It was possible for the team finish 15 points on the last morning of sprint.

Burn down chart chart Velocity chart

The burn down chart demonstrates the progress that the release team makes on a particular project during the course of a sprint from beginning to finish versus the real-time daily progress. The velocity chart shows the estimated effort by story point that can be delivered by a release team to deliver over several sprints.

The goal for the chart's purpose is to aid the scrum master become competent in managing sprints and releases more efficiently daily. chart offers the scrummaster an overview of the general capabilities to manage the developers as time goes by.

The velocity chart is used to determine how many points of work are completed in a sprint for a particular team

It assists the scrum master to monitor and deal with issues that may arise. It helps with more precise sprint planning

Its Burn down chart provides how much outstanding work is compared against the time available. Team velocity charts highlights the work (as numbers) for a team across multiple sprints as well as numerous releases.

Velocity charts for releases show team performance over the sprints within a specific release.

Figure 2a depicts the The chart of Velocity, while Figure 2b depicts the chart of burn down

Chapter 10: Scrum Artifacts

This is a key component of the Scrum framework that you don't wish to leave out. Let's get archeologically for a minute. The terms used in the nomenclature could be the same. However, the significance and role of archeological artifacts don't change when they relate to Scrum. Scrum framework. There are however different frameworks with various ways of application of terms.

What is the meaning of artifacts in archeology? They are objects made by humans. They are the product of human invention. They are artworks that are created as tools to address the problem or an invention designed to inspire.

Similar to similarly, the Scrum framework is built with several artifacts. In essence, there are three major artifacts the Scrum framework defines. They are:

* The Backlog of Products

*The Sprint backlog

* The product incentive

Other artifacts comprise Sprint Retrospectives, and Refinement of Product Backlogs. All of this artifact is numerous times essential to the general usage and operation of the software.

The reason for the artifacts that are part of the Scrum is to enhance transparency and shared understanding of the tasks of a team. Although the Sprint Backlog and Product Backlog is responsible for defining the work to be performed that can increase the value of the work and productivity, the Product Increment refers to the portion that has been completed of the work that was completed for a certain duration or sprint.

The Product Backlog

The Product Backlog is the section that is part of the Scrum project that establishes the an amount of scale. The segment is able to answer the most fundamental question regarding what is the most crucial project to complete the next time? Simply put, Product Backlog can be described as an artifact that is constantly changing that continue to evolve.

The segment functions as guidelines that define the scope for what needs to be completed at each phase during the course of the work. It is crucial to remember that the product backlog remains subject to change, continuous updating and refinement to accommodate the changes that happen due to the dynamic nature of the development of products.

Manage your backlog of products

This is one of the things that Scrum professionals must be acquainted with. It is vital to strive to keep your product backlog as small and manageable. You're likely to encounter three main issues that can be difficult to resolve when you continue to stock your backlog with too many products. These include:

* Uses up unnecessary time

In the event of having more than one item in the product backlog can make the delivery of work more difficult and as a result, a significant amounts of time is wasted. This is due to the fact that the time needed to sort through the items that are piled up in a random fashion in the backlog is usually more than what it takes to organize. Prioritization becomes difficult and there's a higher chance that items will be duplicated.

* Team Progress is not evident

Due to the time spent organizing items in the backlog of product items and the Scrum Team hardly notices progress they achieve. For example the team that completes 20 of 70 items is likely to notice the improvements they have made. However, if a group finishes 20 of 900, they will be disappointed as the sense of achievement and motivation to go on would inevitably decrease.

* Reduces the length of human capital

Imagine a team of five needing to cut out two members to focus on making decisions about items in the backlog of product development. This is not a good idea for speed as well as urgency and success. If someone must spend precious time creating these backlog items for their product and then lowers the chances of having the visibility anticipated to the future right as soon as they begin the task.

To avoid having to face the above issues What should the team do? To effectively manage the backlog of your team's products make sure it is small and avoid having it item-clogged The following steps can help.

Take away items that you can't realistically ever

If you discover that there are things on the product backlog that your team won't likely be able to accomplish It is recommended to remove them as soon as you can from the backlog of product. By doing this you'll be capable of keeping your backlog of product items small and manageable.

While this might be difficult to achieve, and often are accompanied by some unexpected circumstances where you have to prepare for contingency plans leaders should be proactive and think ahead of the team members when coming up with ideas on the spot to help in the situation.

Beware of items that aren't in the moment

Another strategy similar to the one mentioned above is keeping off items from the backlog of product development that the team isn't yet ready for. The product owner would like to work on the items however, is the team actually prepared to work on these items? How soon will the items be required? Are they in the right place to payment for them right today?

If your answer for the second is not yes, then remove them off the shelves. If the answer is yes to the thirdquestion, take them off the shelf and keep off any other items that aren't needed now. If the team isn't ready to tackle them and is not available in the near future, please remove them from the backlog of product.

Instead of creating a clog in your product backlog, make a storage tank where you can keep items on standby up until the time they're ready to be dealt with by your team. This will help make your backlog of products smaller and manageable.

Product backlogs require periodic review

Think of the backlog of products as your wardrobe, where you store your clothes. How often do you go through it? I guess daily. This is what you should do with your backlog of product. If not every day, like you dress your wardrobe or your wardrobe, establish a obligation to regularly (maybe every quarter) look over your product backlog.

Maintaining your backlog of products to the appropriate size is a problem at all. Start a routine review process for checking the expensive and mundane items. In reality the owner of the product can help you with this and assist you in cleaning up, eliminate or relocate items aren't a priority for the team or that don't attract the immediate interest of the team.

Product Backlog Refinement

Before we proceed onto the following Scrum Artifact, it is crucial to discuss the refinement process for the product backlog. Our prior knowledge places us in the mindset the Product Backlog refers to constantly changing artifacts which are never fully completed.

If some artifacts are being worked on it is likely that something was the primary trigger for this work. This is what in which the product Backlog Refinement performs. Thus the term the term "Product Backlog refinement is the work that is performed to continually change. It is evident that Product Backlog refinement is an essential and continuous position in the the Product Backlog since it constantly evolves to meet the needs of the new product backlog.

Sprint Backlog

As Scrum artifacts are, Scrum Backlogs are artifacts of the process. Sprint Backlog refers to a list of tasks that the Scrum group has completed and prioritized to be completed in each Scrum sprint. Typically, at the time of the sprint meeting where the Development team lays out its strategy, the team typically decides on a variety of backlog items. These are usually as user stories. Therefore, the team decides on the necessary tasks to put the final touches to every user story.

Additionally, the spring backlog is able as having two calls to take action. The first is to consider it to be the "How" of the Sprint and the "What" of the Sprint. With the word "What" it refers to the tasks to be accomplished with the help of the group. The "How" refers to the manner in which these tasks should be carried out.

The Sprint Backlog represents a highly clear, well-planned, and real-time overview of the work The Development Team plans to accomplish during the Sprint. This is a single item exempt to the Development Team

In addition to the two key components of 'How' as well as 'What' in the Sprint, Sprint Backlog also is the design of the Development Team for how they will execute and complete this product Increment.

It's all up to the person you are, you can manage your sprint backlog by using any of the software applications specifically designed for Scrum. The Scrum framework also permits you to present your sprint backlog in an Excel spreadsheet or to deploy the defect management system. Below is an illustration of how you can keep track of the backlog of your sprint.

These are the key content from this Sprint backlog:

1. Tasks that were decomposed from user stories, and approved by the Team for the current version.

2. Time estimations or story points for specific tasks.

3. Product backlog refinements in what is the "definition of work accomplished" with respect to the specific task or story.

4. Refinements of the Product Backlog to stories that do not affect your Sprint Goal or require the Product Owner to make a request for an early end to the Sprint.

5. Stories or tasks that are created to the Team to strengthen your present Sprint Goal.

Also, it should be noted that the Team may at the spring Planning stage set forth what is the Sprint Goal and stories accepted for the current Sprint. But, the Team alters and updates assignments and even stories on their Sprint Backlog when they see the need to do this in order to achieve and support the Sprint Goal.

In general, updating the backlog of sprints every day is acceptable. But, when new information becomes available during a sprint, team members are able to update this backlog. Teams may also decide to update their sprint backlog in each day's scrum. Typically, the tasks that are not completed in the schedule is calculated and then put into graphical form using the ScrumMaster The result will look similar to the chart below:

In the diagram of the sprint backlog depicted in chapter 1 what we see is the fact that this team in this case was unable to complete their work in the beginning into the backlog of sprints. However, they still had enough time to finish day 5 of a sprint lasting 25 days.

In the meantime, the product owner needed to add user stories during the sprint, which led to the most significant increase on the chart between the first day to the 25th. The graph is consistently moving and completed the Scrum sprint with a successful end

It is vital that the team collects the correct amount of work that has been completed as well as completed in during the Scrum sprint. The team is also able to change or delete tasks.

Scrum Focus Zones

What should you concentrate on in the Scrum framework?

* Keep an eye on team performance

It is worthwhile to reiterate that it is through teamwork you can see the capabilities and dedication of every participant. In the end, no one appreciates flawless rehearsals. People praise great work.

Therefore, with Scrum you're not looking for a method that can be used the goal of separating individuals in the team. Instead, it seeks to recognize and capitalize on the potential of expertise, knowledge, skills, and knowledge that are in each member in your organization. When doing this, Scrum focuses on team performance and measures corporate performance rather than individual results.

* Comparative Tasks

What is the best way to measure the effectiveness of your team's tasks within your organization? Do you estimate the effort of your team members according to hours worked? It's not likely to yield desired and desired outcomes. Scrum is a completely unique approach that can be used to achieve results.

The system is based by utilizing the idea of estimation relative to task that is based on size and complexity. In other words, a relative estimation works best in estimating the effort of a member. The concept is that if you evaluate the tasks of individuals based on their size and complexity instead of the amount of time spent, the outcome that you get would be less likely to be prone to error.

* Engage Time Boxing

This is a novel method that for project managers as well as expert progress analysts have found extremely useful. Scrum concentrates on gaining efficiency and engagement through time-boxing. This approach evolves the process of assigning tasks to a specific sequence of.

This means that each repetition has a set timeframe within which each task must be completed. This is different from the current models, particularly the Kanban that helps to achieve the speed and commitment by restricting the amount of work that is to work in the process.

* Assess the Team Happiness Indicators

This is an essential aspect of Scrum. The ability to measure the happiness of your team members at the final stage of the project is a notion that is driven by the notion that a teams perform better in subsequent tasks when they show happiness and contentment with the results of the task at moment.

As a leader, therefore it is crucial to identify, appreciate as well as measure and evaluate the most important motivating factors which increase the motivation and well-being of the remainder members of your team.

* Focus on the goal, not the roadmap

Scrum framework is not a reason to disallow the use of a maps when establishing the path of a project. But, a roadmap should serve as a reference and not be a cast in stone sort of thing. With the Scrum method, each sprint is unique and the plan can be altered to meet the goals of every sprint.

In essence, they are at best a sketchy vision. The past performance and lessons played an important role to guide or influence modifications that will take place from sprint to sprint. This results in what's known as velocity in the Scrum system. With velocity teams are believed to determine their capabilities through their past performance.

* Accept the Process Improvement Commitment Approach

Continuous improvement of processes is the primary goal of Scrum. Jeff Sutherland's innovation is based on the aim that every phase of iteration is expected to produce improved results that enhance the final results of previous performances. Process improvement within Scrum is a technique which focuses on improvements to milestones which is technically referred to as Kaizen.

Chapter 11: Scrum Ceremonies

Scrum Ceremonies

Scrum meetings remain the essential elements in an Agile Software Delivery process. They are the gathering and bringing together of the Scrum teams with the intention of completing work in a systematic, orderly way.

Like the name implies, Scrum ceremonies are gatherings that are not solely for the sake of having fun. Scrum ceremonies provide an opportunity for the scrum team to be able to influence, empower and collaborate. They brainstorm, encourage, and support each other to improve and ultimately deliver outcomes.

If scrums aren't effectively managed, they could turn into simply jamboreees, where teams will spend an enormous amount of time chasing around and waste the valuable time on their schedules. They also diminish the reason and importance of their gathering.

Another purpose for which Scrum events are typically held is to help realize and implement some of the Agile fundamental values and principles Some of them include reviews of progress on work customer satisfaction sustainable effort teamwork, efficient communication, and many more.

Although it is essential for a the team to have these events often, there are times when they might not hold them at all, or because the team does not understand the necessity and significance in the moment, or because they have abandoned the fundamental values and fundamentals. It is risky for a team to not have scrum ceremonies.

What is what are Scrum Ceremonies?

Now, let's go over the four scrums and their purpose. they play in the scrum's overall drive. The most important factors that facilitate successful scrums include the objectives, participants as well as tips and techniques.

The best way to begin the section is to state categorically that Scrum is designed to be a easy and light procedure. But, mastering it may become difficult, particularly in the event that its main purpose of being an effective framework for teams of all kinds to resolve complex issues are not considered seriously.

Scrum events provide a forum for these difficult issues to be discussed and solved. They can help broaden the range of discussion and add a touch of elegance to an non-structured frameworks.

It is crucial to keep at heart that the rituals are linked to specific tasks and objectives within the framework of scrum. In a nutshell it is possible to think of scrum events as an excellent agile method that teams deploy globally to create a strategies that can be implemented. The scrum ceremony includes:

1. Sprint Planning

2. Daily Scrum

3. Sprint Review

4. Sprint Retrospective

1. Sprint Planning

Sprint Planning

Like the name implies the term "sprint planning" refers to the arrangement, design, and scheduling to ensure that that the team working on development is properly and well-prepared to reach the goal and finish work each sprint.

When teams meet at the start of a new sprint the goal is usually to plan for the Product Owner and Development team to review the product Backlog that is prioritized. One important aspect to keep in mind is that the product's prioritized Backlog must contain only the elements that your team is likely to be able complete by the time this sprint.

Sprint Planning, also known as the basis for a Scrum ceremony is designed to be a way of engaging in a sequence of productive discussions as well as brainstorming, negotiation, and discussions that eventually result in the creation of an inventory of sprints that includes everything the team is determined to achieving over the course of a only one sprint cycle.

The achievable goals could be called as the sprint goal, which is which is a tangible increase in productivity which can be proved at the end of the sprint. The goals should be endorsed by the team members in general so that they can collaborate towards their achievement.

Who is invited to the Sprint Planning Ceremony?

Simply put that all roles in the scrum must be present. Every one of them plays an significant role to play to play in Sprint Planning facilitation in order to ensure that the deliberations are successful. In actual fact, each Sprint Planning has in attendance the Product Owner, Scrum Master and Development Team.

What is the role of an Owner of the Product do in Sprint Planning?

Alongside the Scrum Master and the Product Owner also has many of the pre-meeting responsibilities and is responsible for preparing all roles of meeting Sprint Planning. For example the Product Owner takes the responsibility of preparing an itemized Backlog and be ready to review it prior to the meeting.

Furthermore the Product Owner must include acceptance criteria, specifications and any other information needed by members of the Development Team that would give the most precise and accurate estimation of the amount of effort and the performance.

Any ambiguities in terms of questions and beliefs which the Development team might have, the Product Owner needs to be aware of and clear. This way they can have a plan for what their team plans to accomplish and what they will achieve during the course of a sprint.

What is the role of Scrum Master?

Scrum Master is accountable for the facilitation of all sessions of Sprint Planning. They perform the role as a facilitator who makes sure that all questions and assumptions that are made by those on the Development Team which answer have been created from the Product Owner have been appropriately addressed. The time, duration of the Q&A sessions, and the closing session are all responsibilities of the Scrum Manager.

and what about the Development Team?

It is important to note that the Development Team is not a participant or observer in Sprint Planning. They are an integral component of the entire meeting. They should be able to judge the validity in the planning and the responses to the product owner. Prepare questions regarding items that will be added to the Product Backlog for the entire sprint.

What is the duration of Sprint Planning?

The duration of the Sprint Planning ceremony depends largely on the duration of your sprint. Therefore, if the duration of the sprint runs 2 weeks, you're Sprint Planning should not last longer than 3-4 hours. For one week-long sprint, your Sprint Planning should last not more than two hours.

2. Daily Scrum

Also known as"the standup for the day," the daily scrum refers to a brief pulse test that not only determines the tasks of the day for the team, but also most importantly, it helps to find all the roadblocks that hinder the team's progress.

Also known as a scrum The scrum meeting provides the team the chance to come together to define what the daily work plan will look like, and identifying obstacles and potential.

What is the need to be included in Daily Scrum?

The aim for the day-to-day Scrum is to primarily do an overview and review of their activities daily. Scrum is a tool which gives the team an opportunity to regularly discuss their progress individually and as a group. It is a

The entire discussion and debate should be directed toward achieving the common target that was established at the start in the course of the sprint. Daily Scrum helps the team to spot work blocks and provide solutions to eliminate the obstacles.

Who decides what to do is being done during Daily Scrum?

The Scrum Master is in charge of removing obstructions to the accomplishment of objectives through Development Team members. Development Team. This can aid the Development team to achieve more and concentrate on the tasks identified as part of Sprint Planning.

The Development team performs every planned task and activity. Even though they participate in the whole Sprint planning process and Daily Scrum asking questions, providing a possible roadmap and other information, the Development Team caries out all tasks post-daily scrum.

Each day during the scrum at the beginning of each day, during each scrum, the Development Team gives answers to the following crucial questions:

What were you doing yesterday?

* What are you planning to do today?

* Are there any obstructions blocking the way?

While the presence for the Product Owner isn't required in the daily scrum, he plays a key role in the preparation of all roles prior to the standup meeting of the day. They are able to prepare responses to any roadblocks or blockers that the team could identify.

How long should a typical scrum last?

In the ideal scenario, as the aim of a daily scrum is review, outline the day's work and pinpoint any obstacles the session should not exceed 15-20 minutes. It can, however, last beyond that according to the work load of the preceding day. However the daily scrum must be short and straightforward to let everyone on the Development Team and other stakeholders to get started early.

3. Sprint Review

In simple words, sprint review is "stakeholders, please give us an assessment of the completed work. It sounds too simple, doesn't it? It's exactly what it means. When it comes to Sprint Review ceremonies, all done work is presented to The Development Team to the stakeholders. But, the product owner and the scrum master Owner aren't exempt from the meeting.

They get together to show the results of the tasks they've completed in a sprint cycle for the stakeholders for their own opinions.

What is the reason behind Sprint Review?

As you must present to your teachers at the conclusion of the term how much you've learned by writing an exams, at the conclusion of each sprint, you will be evaluated.

It's a good idea to bring back the procedure you used to follow in your former school days: just as you were looking to close the academic year there was an opportunity for you could review all that happened. The same rules and procedures are applicable to this.

The platform also offers the opportunity for users to examine what's been accomplished and get a much earlier than later a sense of what is to come. The users can rapidly modify the software that is the product of the efforts from Development team. Development team.

It is crucial to remember that the work that is showcased in the Sprint Review should be shippable in the sense that they are in line with the requirements and the scope of the scope that was established at the start of each sprint. This can boost the stakeholder trust in the team, and especially those in the Development Team gets much of the thumbs-up.

Once again, Sprint Review is not time to get anxious or to shiver as the average PhD student who is preparing for their Thesis defense. No. Sprint Review, which is also known as Sprint

Demo, is an interactive meeting where Development Team displays what they have achieved during the course of the course of a sprint cycle.

It is designed to build confidence and trust that the participants have in the team, which enhances the bond between both participants. It provides a face-to face way for stakeholders to receive early feedback from their customers as well as an objective evaluation of the work performed in the group.

It is important to be performed with a sense of humor since it's intended to demonstrate the value that the completed work can bring to product development. The team must ensure that they take every step to impress outside reviewers and external evaluations

What is the best time to Sprint Review Appropriate?

The team could decide to have Sprint Reviews staged on a informal "Demo Friday" or have it be an organized gathering where everyone sits in a formal setting.

Who must be present?

Everyone! Anyone! Starting from Product Owner Scrum Master and even Development Attendance is essential. This is when all team members show they're ready for the work they're tasked with. The way they perform will show the stakeholders of how proficient or not the whole team is. Additionally, they will be an assortment of management as well as external and internal participants, customers, and developers from different projects.

It is the task of the Scrum Master and Product Owner to engaged in discussions regarding who is expected to be present for the Sprint Review. In a surprising way, it is the case that Sprint Review is more open to participants as opposed to other Scrum events. It's an event that's fluid which allows both an external and internal evaluation on the performance of your team.

How long is it expected to take?

If you consider the time frame for Sprint Planning, then you will be able to estimate how long the sprint review will be. It is recommended that an hour per week during the sprint would suffice. For instance, if you're running for two weeks and you have a two-hour sprint review, then a Sprint Review should be scheduled.

4. Sprint Retrospective

If you're seeking a way to become more technical during Scrum events and sprints, then Sprint Retrospective isn't the right spot for you. Perhaps, you should look into Scrum Planning. But, Sprint Retrospective represents the last stage in the series of scrums during which teams take a look back and do an extensive review of their.

Whereas other scrum-related events and celebrations may provide an unintentionally serious, relaxed mood the Sprint Retrospective makes use of the anti-Aristotelian extreme virtue of giving us a sexy platform. It's a chance for participants to ask questions about the feedback they receive following the presentation of their work. The team then examines the finished work and pinpoint areas that can be enhanced.

What's on the table the team's agenda?

Great question! Once the Sprint Review has been done and all stakeholders and participants have provided their own reviews and comments, teams has to sit down and think about how they can improve their next delivery.

It is during the Sprint Retrospective where the scrum team is able to discuss the things that are working perfectly; identify the ones which require improvement and suggest the best ways to improve delivery. The main questions that the team will often must confront during Sprint Retrospective session include:

What was the best thing that happened during the course of the previous sprint?

* What wasn't going so well?

* What can we change to help improve?

Sprint Retrospective Retrospective Should Cause Change, Not the Blame

Sprint Retrospectives should serve as an opportunity to not play a blame games or blaming an individual for not doing or doing something. Rather it should be a safe room for participants to provide their honest and objective feedback and suggestions.

It is a forward-looking space instead of a retro-looking space. It should, in essence, drive desired and desirable changes to the entire team. In order to achieve this the data, recommendations, and feedback received from members and other participants must be compiled and implemented gradually as needed to improve the team's performance in the future.

Who is the person to reflect on?

Each Sprint Retrospective meeting, there will be the Scrum Master and the Development Team. Are required to attend. While, participation by Product Owners is a voluntary item. Other stakeholders may also be present.

How long is it?

Since it is a session to provide feedback and feedback, Sprint Retrospective sessions should last longer than an Spring Review in terms of time. But, they should not exceed the maximum time of one hour and thirty minutes for a two week sprint. If you're running a one month of sprint, the Sprint Retrospective may be as long than 3 hours.

Below is a chart that shows the duration that is allowed per Scrum ceremony for the duration of a four-week Sprint:

The Summary of the Scrum Ceremonies

Agile is focused on continuous improvement that is gradual and bringing about changes, so all events must be geared towards improving the quality of service. The team must be motivated throughout each of the event to take an evolving approach to their work.

Although the team is expected to be improve, the resources utilized should be improved and the process should be more efficient and effective in order to accomplish more in a shorter amount of time. Naturally, Scrum gatherings are forums where every participant is exposed to the capabilities and possibilities that are contained within the team.

126

Chapter 12: Breaking Down

A Scrum Project

This chapter we'll examine the way the Scrum project is actually implemented and how Scrum can be tested. We are going to take the time to look at the way the process of a Scrum project is initiated, the place it comes from, as well as an outline of various components and phases that make up the process.

We will also examine the primary elements of an Scrum project. This way, you will be aware of the various factors that make a successful Scrum project requires to reach its objectives.

Then, let's start.

What is an Project?

In essence, a project is a momentary process that results in an end-to-end result.

In this way According to that logic, a project is a reaction to a need, or a need that is what has driven those who are affected to find the solution that is permanent through an action that is temporary.

Let's take a look at an example.

Two towns are separated by the river. For people to move across the river from one to another they have to drive around for an hour to travel around the river. The shortest way between the two towns, which involves crossing the river, could take around 10 minutes.

The two towns have agreed to construct bridges that connect both towns to ensure that people from both towns are able to access both sides. Additionally the towns have accepted to cover half the cost of construction of the bridge.

A commission was established comprising members from both towns , to come up with a plan to finish the bridge. Following meetings, the commission has decided on what they want, when they would like it, and an estimate of the amount of time it will be to complete it.

The commission also had meetings with contractors who presented their plans and ideas. After careful review the commission chose one contractor. The contractor started work and constructed the bridge within three months. They

were paid the contract for the construction work ,
but they was also able to sign an agreement to
maintain the bridge. of the bridge.

The project was a big success. the flow between
the two towns increased and investment
increased and everyone emerged with a win.

In this instance we can see the root of the issue
that is caused by an unending river that splits the
two towns, forcing the towns to travel for a long
distance in order to reach the opposite side. In
the end, there was a lack of business as it could
be and people were dissuaded from visiting the
town on the other side.

It was decided to construct the bridge. The first
step was the building of the structure itself. In the
end, construction was completed in only three
months. We don't anticipate the building's
construction to last forever. We anticipate that
the building will end within a certain period of
time , and the finished product to be ready for
delivery.

Therefore the temporary act (the building of the
bridge) was a permanent solution to the issue

(the bridge). This is an excellent illustration of how a project is just an action that is temporary.

However, there is plenty of work involved in the construction of the bridge. There's labor involved and resources (time material, money, time) that are required to make the project happen. So, it's the job of the project managers to make their best effort to ensure that the project yield the results the way it was meant to.

In this case we decided to go with a more reliable output, considering that bridge construction isn't something that is new. Of course, planners and engineers have taken on their own to come up with innovative designs and explore various approaches. Some have been successful and others have not. But the main aspect is that even in an apparent perfected procedure, there's still room to improve and progress.

In those areas in which there is lower certainty (software development biotech, pharma social programs, biotech, etc.) there is more uncertainty. Thus, project managers have to determine the most effective method to provide results as soon as they can and ensure that these results last for the entire duration of their project. This is the place where Agile excels.

Phases of the Project

The typical project is an ongoing process that needs to be followed to finish the project with success. This is a significant consideration because project managers usually attempt to organize procedures in order to reduce as much uncertainty and risk as they can.

While risk is a element of every project, following precise guidelines and in an appropriate framework can help reduce the risk. But, projects generally have a dynamic nature, where everything can go wrong.

So, most projects contain five phases. Let's go over the details of each phase.

1. Planning. The initial phase of every project is planning. In this stage the project manager will sit down with project stakeholders and the project's sponsors to establish what goals are of the project. This is where the parties involved will meet to hammer out contracts and reach an agreement on the scope of work to be

completed, within the timeframe and what the criteria for acceptance of that project are. The next step is the formation of teams.

2. Initiation. The second stage of a project is the preparation tasks that go into getting the project moving. This might include the purchase of equipment, the recruitment of personnel, as well as the purchase of other items required to get the project off the ground. Additionally, discussions could be held with suppliers when required.

3. Execution. This phase is about getting the work done. Therefore, the team members are able to start working and begin the process of moving. Based on the method of project management that you choose, you may see some preliminary results like in the case of Agile or deliverables. However, the results won't be visible until the end of the project, as with traditional approaches to managing projects. This is the time where the goals are able to be realized.

4. Monitor and evaluate. When a project has reached this stage, it's because the final product is released and being tested. This is the time when the finished deliverables will be tested to

determine if they are in compliance with the specifications required prior to accepting finalization of product. This can result in the customer rescinding the final product, and then requesting revisions prior to the final product being accepted.

5. Closing. After the product has been accepted, the project can enter an end-of-project phase. As the project moves into this stage the final adjustments are added to deliverables and the client gives final acceptance of the products. The ribbon is cut and then the applause comes. The final version of the software is made and there are applauses and high fives everywhere. The project team begins to close the loop and then either go on onto the next task or end the project.

The process mentioned above is the normal life cycle of a project. This kind of procedure is usually seen with traditional methodologies for managing projects. In these cases you'll see that acceptance and testing occurs at the conclusion of the cycle of the project. This means that the client is not aware of how it will be like until the completion of the project.

This method opens the way to a myriad of problems because the team working on the project will not be able to determine what will happen once the customer receives the final product. Therefore, there is a real possibility that the customer may not approve of the final deliverables and request changes. If that happens, the situation could cause a major problem for the team working on the project as any changes made to deliverables after they are assembled could cause significant cost and delays. Therefore, ensuring that all final results are made according to the requirements from the clients is vital so that there are no delay or surprise at the conclusion to the task.

What is the role of Scrum Integrate Into All This?

Scrum is executed in the same manner as regular project work. The primary distinction between traditional projects and Scrum is the mindset and attitude towards change flexibility, and harnessing the potential of changes.

Naturally, Scrum begins with a planning phase which then will lead to the initial phase. When the project is completed and in operation then the development team is able to enter and begin working. But the primary distinction between Scrum and Scrum is the fact that its execution phase will be divided into smaller sections known as "sprints." They are intended to be stages that allow the team to create a specific part of the final product. When the sprint, the client will be able to view the entire process being executed, to give an idea of how your final output will appear to be.

Monitoring and evaluation phases is integrated into every sprint so that the team working on the project can evaluate the product and decide whether there are any modifications that must be changed to ensure that everything is working smoothly. In the end, the closing statement will result in the client accepting the final product and thus bringing the project to a close.

Because every project is unique and unique, the team behind the project has to be ready for any situation that might come their way. This involves being open to new possibilities and ensuring they are equipped with everything to be the most successful they will. However, care must be taken to ensure that the most essential elements of the final product are considered.

As you can see, the most significant difference in terms of structure that an Scrum project has , when compared with an old-fashioned one can be seen in the fact that Scrum concentrates on the client, providing value as quickly as is feasible and working out any bugs that might arise right from the beginning. It ensures that all parties are aware of which aspects of the program are progressing.

In addressing any the issues that could arise as early as they can the team on the project can find out if there is any cost or time overruns and determine how they can be dealt with. Additionally, the team can identify what needs to be addressed to avoid time and cost overruns. So the project can be successful, fulfill the criteria for acceptance and meet the stated goals.

Scrum Project Components

We will get into the particulars of the parts that compose the components of a Scrum project.

Let's first take a look at the people who comprise the Scrum team.

The Product Owner. The Product Owner of the Scrum team is referred to as "the Voice of the Customer." What this means is that developers will not have direct contact with the client. It's the job of the Product Owner. This is because the Product Owner will be the primary person responsible for interacting with customers so to ensure that the product owner can convey the vision of the client and their feedback to the other members in the group. This means that the Product Owner sits on the forefront within the creation process. The Product Owner plays a crucial position of leadership, they are not the main boss.

* Scrum Master. The name given to this player is not a reference to "master" in regards to leadership or domain however it is a reference to the degree of expertise within the Scrum method. This is why Scrum Master is the Scrum Master is the link between the Product Owner (the

customer) and the Development Team. The job that Scrum Master is Scrum Master is one of subordinate leadership. This means that the Scrum Master is engaged in providing direction and direction when required, but is not an actual "boss." In reality the job of the Scrum Master is to supply all the essential tools and elements that are required by the Development Team needs in order to achieve their goals.

• Development team. This Development Team is the one who is responsible for setting the project in motion. They are the ones who are actually carrying out the task. A typical Development Team consists of about four to six members. They usually operate in a co-located environment which is to say, at the same physical location under the supervision of the Product Owner and Scrum Master. They are also responsible for coordinating the development team. Development Team is also in charge of delivering product demonstrations and technical explanations for the client, especially in the event that the Product Owner isn't the best qualified to provide the information.

As you will see, the number of participants within the Scrum team is pretty tiny. Therefore, one of the most common criticisms against Scrum is that it's not scalable , particularly for massive and complex projects. This assertion cannot be farther from the truth.

In the case of massive projects, Scrum can be scaled up in such a way that many Development Team teams work in conjunction with several Scrum Masters for the purpose of helping break down the work into smaller, manageable chunk.

In reality, big projects might have additional roles , such as a Project Product Owner as well as the Project Scrum Master. The two roles are responsible for ensuring that all the machinery of the project works together.

While we'll go deeper into the details of Scrum roles in subsequent chapters, it's important to point that the explanation of the roles we've given here can help to get a better understanding of the way Agile and, in particular Scrum perceive the interactions among the different participants throughout the course for the undertaking.

It is important to remember that Scrum is a method of achieving efficiency by achieving the highest quantity of work accomplished using the least number of employees.

Does this mean that employees will be stretched to the limit?

Actually, no.

Keep in mind that Scrum is a method of ensuring an enduring pace. That means it means that the Development Team needs to be challenged to a reasonable level. So, you shouldn't think that to have the Development Team to be working 24 hours a day and keep that speed over a long period of time. Naturally, there will be instances when these things might be required.

In the event that the project is unable to meet time If the project is delayed, the Development Team must work at the fastest pace they can while the Scrum Manager and Product Owner determine the most efficient method to increase the speed and make up the time lost.

Keep in mind that Agile does not permit being behind on schedule. Instead, Agile seeks to deliver ahead of time. Although delivering ahead of time isn't a top priority however, it is more important than getting in the lagging position.

This is the reason both the Scrum Manager and the Product Owner should be aware that pressing on the Development Team to the max is not the ideal method of operation as this could cause the team to burnout and cause many more problems on the job than was originally anticipated.

There is a third person who isn't normally part of a typical Scrum team, but could be brought in if required. The character is known as"Agile Coaching. "Agile coach." The Agile Coach as its name implies is a coach who will help Scrum team members through the correct implementation of Scrum concepts and methods. This coach could come in handy when teams are novices to Scrum and aren't yet fully able to develop the process they require. The Agile Coach is able to "correct" errors and ensure there is a strictness in teams adhere to the Development Team adheres to the guidelines of the Scrum project.

An Agile coach is a professional with experience with all three levels within the Scrum project management area. The ideal candidate for this role is that the Agile coach will have worked as a developer, thereby providing the necessary expertise and understanding of the process the typical Development Team goes through. The Agile Coach can visit and leave as required or be part-time in their Development Team while they learn how to use the Scrum method.

What exactly is what is a "Sprint"?

We have previously talked about the different phases of the project. These are the basic procedure by which breakdown of work occurs within the scope of a project. Therefore, each phase focuses on diverse tasks, which are typically interdependent. So, it is impossible to change from one phase to the next without completing the necessary foundational work. This means that Scrum teams must understand what the tasks of one sprint must be completed to be built upon to the next.

Sprints occur during the execution stage of the project where the work being accomplished is in fact geared towards creating an end product. This is why it is the Development Team takes center stage throughout each sprint. Both the Product Owner and Scrum Master take on an important, secondary function, where they help ensure they are ensuring that everyone on the Development Team has everything they require to complete the task.

During sprints it is rare to have the Product Owner in the actual task being completed except when it is necessary because of unexpected reasons. The person responsible for ensuring that everything runs according to plan is called the Scrum Master.

So it is that Scrum Master Scrum Master can be described as the person who looks at the potential problems could arise and then find innovative ways to address them when they are able to be resolved prior to time. If problems arise that are unavoidable due to any reason, the Scrum Master has to deal with issues, often in collaboration together with the Product Owner so that to allow the Development Team to keep working.

The only reason Development Team members Development Team should stop working is when there is unimaginable events that could cause the project to cease operation. But, to reach an event like this would be a rare event which no one in their reasonable mind could accurately predict.

However, sprints typically run between 2 and 6 weeks , with the typical duration of a sprint being four weeks or a month with the possibility of an hour or two.

The reason for this specific duration of sprints is that four weeks is the best period in order for Development Teams to actually produce results. If sprints are longer, it will be more difficult to achieve accurate results, while having longer sprints could result in time being wasted.

Naturally, due to Scrum's flexibility that if a sprint of four weeks isn't enough for the nature that the team is working on, the Scrum Director and Product Owner might decide to run a longer sprint the next time. If they think there was a surplus of time the work that they had done, it could be included in the next sprint instead of reducing the subsequent one.

It's important to remember that sprints could vary in length over the duration of the project. Thus, you may have a an earlier, three-week sprint in the beginning of the project, and run 5-week sprints at different stages of the project. However but it's not recommended because it might disrupt the development team's pace and rhythm. The best option is to keep sprints' lengths as equal as is possible.

Sprints are built upon repetition. That means that sprints are of the same structure, meaning that every sprint will follow the same procedures and steps executed. What this means is that it provides an element of predictability in how every sprint is run. In light of the fact that Scrum is a highly uncertain and unstable environment, having some degree of predictability is ideal to allow Development Teams to build around.

In the next section, we'll discuss more in depth on the way each sprint operates. The most significant takeaway from this point is that sprints are the primary instrument used to plan the tasks to be completed within a project.

The Project Charter

When working on the course of a Scrum project is completed, it is necessary to create a Project Charter is created during the planning phase.

The negotiation and writing of Project Charter are the responsibility of the Product Owner. It should be written in advance before any of the many components of the project is installed. In reality it is possible that the Project Charter may be written prior to the time that even the Scrum Master and Development Team is established.

What is an "Project Charter"?

When it comes to traditional project management it is an Project Charter would be the contract signed by the client with the organization that is in charge of executing the project. This is why Scrum is not a proponent of an actual contract however, rather, it is a document that reads like an Memorandum of Understanding in which all the basic guidelines are laid out for the management of the project.

Thus it is expected that the Project Charter will contain everything that pertains to the duration and scope of work, its deliverables and acceptance criteria, as well as details of payment, and any other requirements that the stakeholders consider necessary and relevant.

The Project Charter, in itself is not legally binding. It is, instead, an act of good faith which enables all participants to understand the guidelines on which aspects of the program will be managed. This is in line with the fundamentals of Agile that emphasizes the use of software over complicated documentation.

There will now probably be a requirement for legally binding, formal contracts. In such a scenario it is the responsibility of the Product Owner will consult the appropriate legal counsel to be responsible for drafting contracts that are based on the Project Charter. It is the obligation for the Owner of the Project to write the Project Charter, it is not the responsibility of the Product Owner of drafting contracts , unless they are licensed lawyers.

It is essential that the Project Charter must then be approved by the client or stakeholder(s) who are coordinating the project. After approval this Project Charter comes into force and is the official document to guide the development of the project.

Since there isn't a formal template to create the Project Charter, I recommend making it similar to a Memorandum of Understanding in which it is stated explicitly that all the participants within the project are in agreement with the provisions in the document and pledge to adhere to these throughout the duration of the project. Additionally, there should be clauses that address the resolution of conflicts. Although you wouldn't be anticipating a conflict to arise but you must ensure that it is included to ensure that all parties are protected should there ever be any type of dispute between the parties.

The Project Charter, as the law of the land should be discussed with everyone on the Project Team so that they know what they must accomplish and how they are expected to accomplish it. The Product Owner could make mini charters outlining the roles of every participant on the Development Team. This is an effective tool particularly when there are instances of Development Team members unclear whether an activity falls within their realm and responsibilities or not.

User Stories

Another one of the primary duties is the creation of"user story" or "user tales."

The user's story provides a thorough explanation of the needs of each component of the project to assist the team in coming with the best solution. Thus the user story is like giving a name and persona to the people who are going to gain from the initiative.

Let's look at an illustration.

The primary product of the project will be a fitness mobile application. The app will monitor health-related statistics like the amount of steps taken or time spent in the gym, food habits, and so on. The project was launched with the signing of a Project Charter signed and approved.

The product owner is currently in the information gathering stage where the client has stated what they want but they're not certain of what the product will look similar to. Additionally, they are not certain of the people their primary customers are.

So, it's up to the Product Owner to create the user's story, in accordance with what the user has stated. Accordingly, the client's specifications require that the application to be targeted towards young adults who work in high-speed environments and have little of time and focus on fitness. The application is designed to give reminders to drink enough water, taking breaks to stretch and the like.

In this regard the Product Owner could develop an account of the user that explains who this particular user will be. Thus, a story of a user may look something like this:

"Joe is a 28-year old bank worker who is working 12-hour days. He is a single man who has a dog at home in his small apartment in the city center of a major metropolitan city. It is a walk to work each day since his workplace is just fifteen minutes from his home. He prefers walking rather than using public transportation as the walk lets him gain exercise. He is a health-conscious person, but isn't always able to stick to an exact diet. He is also extremely technologically adept. He will use his smartphone for almost anything he needs to do."

This story of a user is only an example. It can be more specific. The more the amount of detail, the better information it can provide to for the Development Team in creating the application with these features in mind. User stories may also be specific in describing features, such as:

"As an user, I'd like to track how many steps I've walked every day, and how it compares to the previous days, so I can keep track of my exercise, to help me shed weight."

After an Owner of the product has come up with the user's narrative, the user is able to look over the story and make suggestions or approve it. If the customer is satisfied with the product then the Product Owner is in the process of getting in motion for the development of the app.

There are some twists in this scenario the Product Owner can decide to complete the entire process of writing user stories on their own or employ the Scrum Master to develop it. Another possibility is that the Product Owner employs members of his Scrum team to create the user stories in an integrated team process. This is a great option, especially if the Product Owner doesn't have much knowledge of the product that is being created.

It is important to remember it is the responsibility of the Product Owner to ensure that they doesn't have to have a degree on the product that is that is being created, but they do need to be a skilled Scrum practitioner. Scrum Master Scrum Master should at least be aware of what the product's features are and what the development process looks like. The people who are experts on the product that is being created are participants of the Development Team.

A final word on user stories: these stories are based on actual users who will be using the product after it's launched. So the Product Owner could decide to speak to prospective customers to gauge the features they'd like. It could involve focus interviews, group discussions and any other type of investigation needed to gather the information required to develop a convincing user-centric story.

Acceptance Criteria

The final component of the Scrum plan is the criteria for acceptance the client has defined to establish the quality of the product. If the requirements for acceptance are not met, the Scrum team has to go back to figure out the issue. It is important to note that the criteria for acceptance are considered throughout the entire process of development. So it is important that you and your Development Team keeps these parameters in mind it shouldn't pose any issues when it comes to achieving the acceptance requirements.

Acceptance criteria may come through specific functions that the software offers. It can be written as a checklist or part of the story about the user. In the earlier example, we spoke about the fitness app. Therefore an example of acceptance conditions for this fitness application could include:

"Given I've completed 10,000 steps, when I reach this goal I receive a notification via an app."

Other acceptable criteria include automated reminders for medications and vitamins. This could also include audio alerts that say "it's the time for you to take a sip of more water." Of of course, this is something the client specifies, and the Development Team must produce.

Also, it must be remembered to note that Development Team should not produce something that the customer has not requested by the customer. This means avoiding the temptation to "improve" on the customer's suggestions.

Why?

Features and functions that are not requested could cause unnecessary work. The client may not like the new features or even ask why it was introduced in the first instance. This could lead to a waste of time and money. Any "improvements" need to be discussed with by the Development Team through the Scrum Master to ensure that the Product Owner is able to talk to the client and explain exactly what Development Team wants to do and why they are planning to implement it.

When the customer knows what is going to be accomplished and the reasons for doing it Once the customer is aware of what needs to be done, the Development Team can proceed with confidence. This is the kind of continuous communication that both sides have to keep in place. Naturally, as nobody is perfect There are situations that were not considered in the beginning of the project but were discovered during development. Thus you and the Development Team can bring up their concerns and problems and let them be heard.

The acceptance criteria are laid out as part of the Project Charter and can be included as a checklist to the benefit of the Development Team. Based on these user storylines, the acceptance requirements, and the features requested by the client they and Development Team can work together to decide on the best way to meet the criteria for acceptance and create the outcomes.

Because Scrum Teams are self-governing and self-governing, the Development Team itself can decide the way they will approach the creation of their product. The Scrum Master can only act as a moderator throughout the process, and keep track of the requirements to complete the task completed.

All the details regarding the task to be accomplished will be clearly displayed within the Scrum Burndown chart. The Scrum Master, and in particular the Product Owner, will work in the background, making sure that everything is in line to the schedule.

In the next chapters, we'll go into more specific details about the process of an entire sprint and how each participant interacts with each other. Additionally, we will give some examples that will assist you in understanding how Scrum projects are executed in a typical everyday context.

Chapter 13: The Scrum Core And Non-Core Roles

There is nothing strange or unusual about the concept of Scrum Roles. It's the everyday usage of roles within our workplaces. Here's the difference the scrum roles focus on the team, not individuals.

They represent the role that individuals play in the achievement of a an overall goal. Within scrum there exist fundamental groups that perform specific duties related to project management as well as software development. They are the product owners the scrum master and the development team.

Let's look at all of Scrum essential tasks.

1. The Product Owner

It is true that there is no construction without a builder and, as such that no project can be executed in an absence. Like the name implies, the owner of the product has the title of the individual who controls the product. Perhaps, this sounds like a like a circular process. In Scrum the product owner is the representative of both the business and the client for the product they are working. The owner of the product has access to the backlog. They decide what items will are more important over others. They set the pace for every sprint or iteration. They strive to prioritize things to be tackled.

The market survey and industry to discover the needs and expectations of customers and make educated executive decisions about product every day. Through this process, they aid in translating those demands into tangible work tasks that can be implemented by Development. Development team.

2. The Scrum Master

While a group wants work to be completed faster and with a taste workers must be equipped with all the tools they require to accomplish this aim. There are employees and those who are accountable for making things work.

A Scrum master is part of the second category. The person in charge is who is responsible for making sure that the team is equipped with all the tools they require to provide worth. The scrum master can be a facilitator, coach or moderator. They could also be a motivator, moderator advocate, counselor, mediator or mediator.

The Scrum master should be one who can project into the future, anticipating obstacles before they develop into project obstacles. Therefore, he's an obstacle remover.

He assists in making sure that there is continuous and seamless communications channels between the participants of the group. As an advocate for the team, the Scrum master is the intermediary between the teams working on development and the owner of the product.

He is the mediator to ensure that all the facilities needed are in place prior to when they're needed. In actual fact the Scrum master oversees all aspects of scrum; he's the scrum project manager. Therefore, whatever duties and tasks you believe a project manager is expected to perform the scrum master must.

3. The Development Team

The process of delivering a working software is not a joke. It is not only vision, but also to be led by a group. A development team is an organization of cross-functional and multi-purpose team members that are focused on ensuring the successful delivery of functional software.

The Development Team, also called the Scrum Team, consists of all those who are involved in the technical aspects of the project. It includes professionals, novices in software development experienced, experts, novices designers, and QA who with the development of the product.

Typically, the development team is comprised of between 5 and 10 people who are completely committed to executing a scrum project. However, things can change the process and in this case, agencies may choose to adopt a different method in response to the challenges they face.

In any event, ideal the development team, assisted by the Scrum Manager and Product Owner is a self-organizing, motivated group of people who can provide the value.

Non-core Roles

The non-core roles are those that are not essential or essential for scrum projects to function effectively. These roles are made up of individuals who are want to participate in this project from an outsider's perspective. They do not participate directly in the day-today running or execution of the project. Contrary to the core roles the roles that aren't core have no formal function they can play with respect to this scrum-related project.

They can assist and communicate with the team, but they do not hold any official obligation to the successful completion in the course of the work. They do, however, as we've discussed in previous discussions, provide a third-eye to keeps the team on their toes so that they can achieve an optimal results. Therefore, the roles that are not core must be considered when the team makes a decisions about what to do with Scrum project.

The continuity of their roles can be terminated in any moment but it's not recommended to eliminate individuals who are not essential in any project. In the Sprint Review session, the people who are involved are vital when it comes to providing feedback and ensuring the team continues to improve the work they are able to show.

The non-core roles that are part of the scrum project are:

1. Stakeholders

When we say stakeholders, we are referring to various concerns. It's a term used collectively which refers to the range of people who are willing to participate in the project. Some participants participate in the project solely as users, while others are sponsors. The key stakeholders of the Scrum project are users, customers, and sponsors.

They are constantly in contact directly with Product Owners, Scrum Master and Development Team. The role of these people, even though they have no formal, role is providing the key roles members with valuable insights which can aid in the improvement of the projects that are presented. They also assist in the creation of the project's service, product or other product.

Stakeholders are another important group who can influence the project through its development phases. They have a significant role to play in various stages such as Develop Epic(s) and create a Prioritized Product Backlog, Perform Release Planning, and then Retrospect Sprint.

Chapter 14: Scaling Scrum

Disclaimer!! !

The first thing you should say as a warning before you begin to think about the concept of scaling Scrum If scaling is a solution, will it solve my problems. If not, then don't. This sounds intimidating, don't you think? But it's not as scary as you imagine. It's important to ensure that the warning is given earlier to ensure that you don't have to regret something you could be avoiding.

Let's get that out of the way for our minds, but keep it in an end of our minds in the process of trying to talk about the mechanics for scaling Scrum.

The primary purpose that scaling has is solve problems related to the agility of Agile methods or Scrum frameworks. In the present, there are several agile frameworks that can scale and are specifically designed to tackle the issues. The frameworks that are scaling are Nexus, Spotify model, Scrum at Scale, Large-Scale Scrum (LeSS), Scaled Agile Framework (SAFe), and Disciplined Agile, in addition to other. Based on the framework you choose the framework you choose operates in a different way and has an approach that is focused on.

Scaling Scrum Frameworks

1. Large-Scale Scrum

Large-Scale Scrum is a framework that is used by multiple teams to scale agile development and projects. Its operation is based upon a set of fundamentals that offer simple structure, guidelines, and rules. The principles focus on the use of Scrum for large-scale product development

The framework performs better and is an ideal start for a team which already has Scrum established. It's an excellent scaling framework for medium and small teams. Therefore, if you're looking to expand your teams, then you need to choose LeSS. However, the scaling must be only one team at a.

LeSS's features LeSS

* Researches the mechanism of empiricality self-managing and self-motivating teams, organizational design and theories of constraints

the concept of systems, lean waste and the theory of queuing.

* Provides guidelines and structures to adopt Scrum for large-scale product development.

* Scales up using minimal extra steps, and is not a one-team Scrum.

* Suitable for medium and small scrum scaling solutions

* Setting agendas to help achieve the Scrum's mission

2. Scaled Agile Framework (SAFe)

SAFe is a new method to increase the scale of Scrum. It is an interactive framework based on knowledge SAFe was designed to be used by large-scale organizations. It's designed to implement agile practices at the enterprise or large-scale levels. The framework comes with lots of guidelines that covers a broad range of subjects, such as financing as well as enterprise architecture.

Chapter 15: The Scrum Framework

The Scrum framework is one which needs to be modified to the environment the environment it is used. It's not a system which tells the development team what they should do but rather specifies what is required to be accomplished. It is the Scrum framework is flexible and allows team members in the Scrum group to prioritize their work and sketch out the roadmap for the product as a team initiative.

If it is used properly, Scrum can help a development team create high-quality products, by maximising their time and efforts. Scrum is implemented by allowing the team to self-organize which means that each member is accountable of their own role in the creation for the product.

For the best chance of success with the Scrum implementation There are guidelines, procedures, roles assignments and values that must be followed.

Scrum Team

There are three primary roles that play a role in a small Scrum team that is typically not more than 9 to 10 members. The team has to remain small to be able to work together and usually within the same area or at a minimum, it should have online tools that keep the group members on constant contact with one another.

The primary duties include:

Development Team

The development team is made up of developers who are experts who are capable of managing their work and working together with their team members to ensure that they all work towards the common aim.

Specific characteristics for the Development Team

• Responsible and confident enough to be able to maximize their workload when they are able by their organization to do so.

They are cross-functional experts that allow them to tackle every aspect of the product's advancements.

Whatever their job is each developer has the same title so that all developers are equally distributed across the entire team.

* Acknowledges that responsibility for the project is entrusted to the entire team group, regardless of abilities.

It is only the team that develops has the authority to make an increment, and everyone on the team has to accept this increment "Done'.

Product Owner

The Product Owner is responsible for the responsibility of making sure that the Backlog of Products meets the requirements and needs of the company or user of the system in the development. They must ensure the quality of the product that is developed by the team of developers.

The characteristics of the owner of the product

* They can be capable of making an organized product backlog.

* They are accountable for ensuring that the Backlog Items are correctly arranged and perform

169

a function or attribute that adds importance for the products.

* Keep the Product Backlog updated and accessible for everyone to view at all times.

* They should ensure that the team working on development is aware of every item on the product's board.

Scrum Master

The Scrum Master acts as the referee of the team. They have to ensure that everyone understands the rules, adheres to the principles and ensure all members have the resources and tools necessary to accomplish their objectives.

The Scrum Master is responsible for ensuring that the product stays within the guidelines and should be the person to resolve any issues or iterations that don't stay on course. The Scrum Master will assist and guide the team during the course of the project.

The Scrum Master must manage diverse interactions between members of the development team and the stakeholders. He guides the team through the many changes and interactions that will add value to the product being created.

Scrum Master Scrum Master, as a matter of fact is a person who is a person who serves 3 groups.

Scrum Master interactions in conjunction with Product Owners

* Ensures that the objectives in the Backlog for Product are clearly stated and well understood by all members of the team.

* Aids the Product Owner in finding methods to effectively manage backlogs of products.

* Aids the Product Owner to organize the Product Backlog so that it's impact is maximized to generate value.

* Aids the Product Owner to facilitate requests for events.

Scrum Master interactions in conjunction with Development Team

* Ensures that all purposes of the product are clearly stated.

* Aids the development team self-organize.

* Facilitates the occurrence of events that require immediate action at the time they arise.

* Ensures that the Daily Scrum runs when planned and seeks out effective solutions to problems that might have been triggered.

Scrum Master Interactions with the Stakeholders/Organization/Customers

* Coaches the team according in line with how to implement the Scrum framework.

* Helps to plan the Scrum implementation with the help of the organization/stakeholders/customers.

* Collaboration together with fellow Scrum Masters in the organization to ensure the efficacy of Scrum throughout the company.

Scrum Values

To allow Scrum to benefit the company in the long run, the Scrum team has to be able to be committed to learning and follow those five Scrum values. These values form the three pillars of Scrum which include transparency as well as inspection and adaptation.

5 Benefits of Scrum

1. Engagement

Every team member is committed to working hard to achieve their goals , and in this, they achieve the objectives of Scrum.

2. Courage

Each member of the team has to show they are able to endure tough circumstances or difficulties and always be a good person.

3. Focus

The focus of each team member should be on the primary goals of the Sprint in order to accomplish the ultimate objectives that are the goal of members of the Scrum team.

4. Openness

Communication must be transparent between team members, the management, and other stakeholders. Any roadblocks or issues should be reported and any challenges be brought to the appropriate parties to be brought to the attention of.

5. Respect

Every member of the team must respect and respect the team members and what they can contribute to the team.

Scrum Rules

To achieve the objectives of Scrum There are twelve fundamental rules to be followed in order to make sure development is running efficiently, squanders any wasted time, and provides the desired product.

12 Fundamental Rules of Scrum

1. The Sprint Planning' meeting each Sprint.

2. The "Sprint Planning" session is time-blocked, typically up to 2 hours for each meeting.

3. Each Sprint should have the same amount of time.

4. There should not be any interruptions between sprints. After one sprint is completed the previous

sprint, the next one must begin after the scheduled Sprint meeting.

5. Each Sprint should be planned with the goal of demonstrating the application at the conclusion each Sprint.

6. A Daily Scrum is to be conducted each day throughout during the entire duration of the work.

7. Daily Scrum: Daily Scrum must be timeboxed to 15 minutes or less.

8. After each Sprint There is the Sprint review.

9. Sprint Review Sprint Review should be timeboxed to two hours.

10. It is recommended to hold an Sprint Retrospective meeting after every Sprint Review. A new Sprint should begin without the Sprint Retrospective.

11. It is recommended that the Sprint Retrospective meeting should be scheduled for 2 hours.

12. Scrum Master Scrum Master is accountable for making sure everyone adheres to the Scrum guidelines.

Scrum Events

Scrum uses scheduled activities to minimize the need for urgent meetings that aren't scheduled into the already strict agenda of the day.

Every Scrum event is timeboxed meaning that it's assigned a time limit to the end of the event or a certain amount of time. Anything that's not completed or announced in that timeframe must be moved or put off. Similar to pre-determined dimensions of boxes for packing, in the event that an item doesn't fit into the container, then it should be moved to the next box or assessed whether it's needed even at all.

Sprint

Sprints are the main Scrum event. Sprint is the most important Scrum event and is governed by strict rules for the process of planning, developing and closing of an Sprint. It also has a suggested method for cancelling the Sprint.

The Scrum framework is built around the idea of breaking down a project into smaller, manageable tasks. The purpose of a Sprint is to publish at a minimum a functional demonstration or functional part within the scope of project. Once the Sprint has been completed, it's designated as "Done" in the team of developers. All need to agree with the Sprint is completed.

Each Sprint will have each of its own project plan that outlines the things being planned as well as the method by which it is to be created and the length of time it will take to complete it.

Every Spirit needs to have the ability to adapt and change to any moment during the life of the Sprint.

Each Sprint is limited to taking no more than one months (30 days) to be completed. If the Sprint will take longer than this the Sprint must be further broken down.

Each Sprint, There Should be the following events:

* Sprint Plan

This is where the entire planning for the Sprint is made. Here, the Development team works with the Sprint team to decide the features that are required in the Sprint.

Sprint planning comes with a time limit that can be set at 8 hours. The meeting is conducted under the direction of the Scrum Master, who is responsible for all the proceedings.

The Product Owner is responsible for ensuring that the team understands the objective for the Sprint and is in line with the needed features.

In the course of this meeting, group discuss topics like:

Which items of the Product Backlog can the team include into the Sprint?

* What steps will the team take to finish the work to finish the Sprint?

* The purpose is the purpose of Sprint.

* Daily Scrum

It is a daily time-boxed event lasting between 15 and 20 minutes in which every team member is required to attend. This is where the tasks for the day are scheduled and discussed in order to ensure that every team member is to the right path.

In this meeting, the team works together to solve any issues that could have arisen on in the past. The team members leave the meeting with a clear idea of the distance they're to finishing the project, or Sprint.

The daily meetings have demonstrated to increase the chances for being able to ensure that both Sprint and the overall project being done on time and according to the highest standards.

* Sprint Development

This is where the actual development work is done by a group comprised of highly skilled people. Every member of the team works towards an end goal that is common to all team members: finishing the project within the timeframe and meeting the project's demands.

* Sprint Review

At the conclusion of every Sprint The team, along with stakeholders conduct an Sprint review in which the product is reviewed. The team can show stakeholders the outcomes that was achieved during Sprint Development. Sprint Development and also ensure that they are aware of the features that went in the Sprint.

At this meeting where the team discusses how they can optimize their next Sprint and outlines what they can do in the following Sprint to maximize the effectiveness of the next Sprint.

The product is usually discussed at this time in order for the team to receive useful feedback from participants and to plan any modifications or adjustments to the Sprint which may be required. In certain instances they will decide whether or whether the Sprint is even needed particularly when something has changed within the project since last Sprint Review.

* Sprint Retrospective

The Sprint team gathers for up to a two-hour meeting to discuss the ways they can enhance the following Sprint. The meeting occurs immediately following an initial Sprint Review and prior to when the next Sprint begins.

Every Sprint is evaluated with respect to the individuals who developed the Sprint to assess how they did their job and any issues that could be avoided for the following Sprint.

The team talks about any additional tools that might be required or processes that can be improved or teamwork issues that require to be improved.

The meeting is monitored by the Scrum Master to ensure that the meeting is productive one and doesn't go beyond the allotted time limit.

Scrum Artifacts

An Scrum Artifact is an item designed to provide worth to the process, and keeps a record or clear information for everyone to view to determine the progress of the project.

Scrum Artifacts comprise:

Product Backlog

A Product Backlog can be described as a list of requirements or wish list that comprises the entire system that must be planned, developed, and then implemented by a highly skilled team of Scrum Developers.

It is solely the responsibility of the Owner. He or she must manage and assure that any changes or patches, as well as new features, etc. are noted in the order they are requested for.

The Product Backlog is added to as needed and is able to be ordered, prioritized and later re-ordered and prioritized. The Product Owner has to be aware that the list is not completely comprehensive.

The product Backlog list is maintained long after the initial project has been completed because there are always requests for bugs and updates, upgrades, etc.

Sprint Backlog

Conclusion

Being a competent team or project leader is essential to ensure the successful execution of any kind of project. With technological advancements that are at a rapid pace, it's business suicide to not implement efficient systems to help an organization keep up in the direction of.

While traditional methods might have worked at their time, they pose a risk rather than reap rewards. The way in which an organization handles these changes could help them stand out from their competitors because they can show that they have the capacity and know-how to create superior quality systems in shorter time-to-market.

With Scrum and the Scrum Framework, a company is able to adapt it within its existing frameworks to increase value and improve the quality of its products as well as its delivery. With the'more working in less space' concept, it minimizes risks cost, as well as ensuring that the entire production team remains involved.

Breaking a big project into small pieces makes sure that any issues are addressed regularly.

Scrum Framework Scrum Framework can be adapted to be used for more than just software development. And it is, in fact, being used by companies like the automotive, military and service companies, and others have been modifying the framework.

It is an agile framework that can be utilized when projects have strict deadlines, complicated features, special requirements, and flexible structure that can accommodate regular adjustments.

It is further improved by combining and leveraging the diverse techniques from other Agile frameworks like Extreme Programming. Scrum has a success in improving productivity and quality, morale of employees and customer relationships.